HAPPYENDiNGS

Vol I

HAPPY ENDiNGS

LOVE DOES WIN

written and authored by

MONI'SOI HUMES

aka #lovegoddess

COPYRIGHT PAGE

© 2016 by Moni'soi Humes

All rights reserved according to UCC 1-308. No part of this publication may be reproduced, distributed, or transmitted in any form or by any means, including photocopying, recording, or other electronic or mechanical methods, without the prior written permission of the publisher, except in the case of brief quotations embodied in critical reviews and certain other noncommercial uses permitted by copyright law. For permission requests, write to the publisher, addressed "Attention: Permissions Coordinator," at the email address below under Orders.
Heaven on Earth, Inc {Publishing}

Ordering Information:
Quantity sales. Special discounts are available on quantity purchases by corporations, associations, public relation & advertising agencies, and others. For details, contact the publisher at the address above.

Orders by U.S. trade bookstores and wholesalers. Please contact Heaven on Earth, Inc., Publishing Department: mhumes@live.com rbragency@gmail.com or visit Author's website www.monisoihumes.co

Booking the Author for speaking engagements, events, and book signings. Email rbragency@gmail.com Printed in the United States of America Publisher's Cataloging-in-Publication data
Moni'soi Humes

Happy Endings/ Vol I. Love does win/ Moni'soi Humes;
ISBN-13:ISBN-13: 978-0692629970 (Heaven on Earth, Inc)
ISBN-10: 0692629971

1. The main category of the book —Relationships —Love- Printed in the United States of America

Dear God,
Thank you for your spirit + this awesome universe.

#LOVEWINS

I dedicate this book to my father, Robert Jones. Fathers matter whether they make good decisions or bad ones. You are an important part of who I am today! This book took courage for moi to write.

I love you Daddy!

There are so many awesome powerful individuals that helped moi embrace loving myself more.

"I love you at your darkest, yet most fearful place in your life. There is no fear in love, but perfect love casts out fear."
-God

"If you walk out the door feeling good about yourself, that's what counts."
-Sarah Jessica Parker

"Sometimes to lose balance in love is to gain balance in life"
Eat. Pray. Love

"Raise the Bar a Little Higher"
-**Sophia Amoruso #BossBabe Founder of Nasty Gals**

"Focus on what you want first, who you are, and what you love. Do what you have to do in order to be in the seat that you want to be in."
-**Beyonce**

"Spirituality is living your life with an open heart through love."

-Oprah {Life Class}

"You learn more in failure than you do in success."

-Jay Z

"I don't do shit until I meditate. Surround yourself with people who are smarter than you."

-Russell Simmons

"We needed love before we fell in love, and we will need it as long as we live."

-Gary Chapman {Author of The 5 Love Languages: The Secret to Love that Lasts}

"Forgiveness is the gift that you give yourself."

-Tony Robbins

preface

about the love goddess

about happy endings

words to know

introduction

chapter 1 ashley madison effect

chapter 2 love & sex

chapter 3 for better or worse

chapter 4 ladies let's give our guys what they want

chapter 5 love is perfected through patience

chapter 6 stop being a modern day jody

chapter 7 empire

chapter 8 without trust you have nothing

chapter 9 shut up & drive

chapter 10 if it ain't about the money, don't be blowing moi up

chapter 11 it takes two to make a thing go right

chapter 12 make sure god is the third cord in your relationship

chapter 13 the heart

chapter 14 stop being selfish

chapter 15 is google a relationship expert
chapter 16 if you have the prize, shut the f up
afterword
author bio
find the author online

preface

this preface was written with no capitalization to show you that you can do, be, and love whomever you want especially your own ways of being peculiar.

"break every chain of anything or anyone who works to confine you to anything outside of yourself"

the choice to love is also your choice to trust. some of us just need to accept the fact that you just need to throw out the ideas, the thoughts, and the misconceptions of love. throw out the lies you were told and taught. stop believing that you will not be blessed if you have not made righteous decisions with your life. yes these are misconceptions, also another way for you to live your life in fear verses a life lived with love. what's right for you could very much be right under your nose, but if you are looking for an idea of love, you will more than likely miss out on the truth of it. your ability to trust will not only change how you have viewed love in your past, it will create a new, right now way of living.

The best love is not confined to one way of doing anything. period! there will be individuals that come in your life and tell you that there are many ways of doing things, but the truth is we all go through bull shit and if we look back at the bs it is enough to laugh about. i just decided to write about the bull shit that i went through. I know there are so many others who are out there going through something similar. people just want to know that someone else is going through what they are going through and that they have already made it through a similar situation.

we all desire to have love the way that we want it. we take so much advice seeking to heal and fix our brokenness in a relationship. it hurts later when the advice you took has caused you to lose what you have based off what another person's opinions of what they think righteous love is. the question we should be asking ourselves is, *"why are we not listening to our own godliness?"* love only desires one thing from us and that is to accept it as the gift that it is. our love is our virtue. it is not our ability to be perfect, nor is it our ability to live without flaws.

it is not for any of us to judge what that means for anyone. your sister may be with a ghetto man, vise versa. you mom or dad may be with a stick in the mud. your best friend may have chosen to spend her life with the wealthiest person on the planet, and your uncle may have fallen in love with the coco. ijs! if he did fall in love with the coco pray for him. people make choices based off of their own needs and desires. their choices are not predicated on anyone around them. they are living for themselves not for you. so many individuals end up with broken hearts spending time forcing their mates to be righteous verses loving them and trusting in who they are to make their own right choices. there is no human being made to live under the telescope of anyones ideas of them living in perfection even if it keeps the person that they love in their life. *love lacks force, when it is love it comes in the form of freedom.*

there are so many controlling individuals in the universe that by the time one receives real love they don't know how to receive it or they question it. people are so use to the spirit of jealousy and envy operating in their lives that when they meet someone who does not have these ill ways about them, they find it hard to deal with them. we often become what we don't like. when someone loves you they are not envious or jealous of you. in reality you are a unite, the two of you are one.

change has been waiting on you

this book was written with the purpose to give you hope, make you laugh, and to share with you some real ass shit. it is about the funny shit that i have been through, my ups, my downs, and the shit that I observed from watching others. if you read anything that you feel you want to apply in your own personal life feel free but there is no obligation to follow anything written in this book. just enjoy it. enjoy your happy ending thoroughly.

sometimes we fail at life, love, and
relationships before we are anywhere near
the success of love and that is completely
ok

IF YOU PROVIDE THE FIRE, THEN I WILL PROVIDE THE SACRIFICE. FILL ME UP GOD!

-Casey J

Dear Sarah Jessica Parker,
To all those #CarrieBrashaws & #MrBigs,

Photo Credits: Photographed by Annie Leibovitz, Vogue, June 2008

Thank you for being an awesome Carrie Bradshaw. You played this role with such fierceness that every time I saw you I could relate to your emotions as Carrie. You have allowed women all over the world to feel your heart in this role in such a way that it was ok for every woman to not only release the lioness in her but to release the pretty little girl from within that loves with every part of her. Your role gave women the strength to love again and to trust that true love exists and it will be there waiting only when they ready to embrace their own purpose as a woman being completely happy with who you are from the inside to the outside.

What I truly admire is that in real life you are truly a woman with your own flair for fashion and a true boss.

To all those Mr. Big's out there, please don't feel like this book is just for the women there is just as much in here for you. If you are a Mr. Big thank you so much for not being afraid to show your Carrie how much you love her. She truly appreciates and values every bit of it from the bottom of her heart. She does not want to go a day without her Mr. Big.

Continue to be a power couple and build your powerhouse from the foundation with love. Rock this world.

That's my best friend,

"Trust is the centerpiece of a relationship, without trust it will not survive. Love is the heart and trust is it's breath."

Anonymous

You are probably wondering why I would write this book and out of all things the topic of love, life, and relationships. Well the answer is pretty simple, in the world of success we have many guides, tools, rule books, and manuals of how to win at being successful. We are told that no matter what we go through that if we remain faithful and persistent with the vision that we started it will work out regardless of what we have to go through. The problem is that no one tells you this when it comes to love, life, and relationships. It is very hard for many people that have to endure tough times in their life, that desire to have a successful relationship that is beyond the tv version of everything that looks good on the outside. People desire to know what works. I am in no way insinuating that I know everything that works, however I am just sharing my side of the story.

There is hope for all those who desire to have it in their life. Hope is our way of holding on, pursuing a life of purpose, and a journey to freedom. Hope is what we have that will lead us to a *"Happy Ending"* in addition to you living a very successful life. Life will awaken you with this incredible energy when you are ready to receive it.

I have learned so much in my life as a writer + a person who loves from the very sound of affirming words. To know moi is to love moi. I am very thankful to a very special person who has been a friend in my life for years. Thank you for being a listening ear, a guiding light, and for awakening a huge giant inside of my small body.

I am honored enough to have someone bold enough to speak to my own enemies, to tear down my own walls of false imaginations, to tell moi that there is a giant that is all so powerful in moi awaiting for more increase. I am very thankful to you for being a person that was willing to split my heart down the middle, shine some light in it, and for literally forcing moi out of my own darkness into the arms of love inside of myself that I may truly love again. I will always love you with all my heart for loving moi and being one of my closets friends in the time of need. You have been there for moi plenty of times never expecting anything in return, but my friendship.

    Love is such a beautiful gift, for now I know that love does not exist without trust. Genuine love will open you up to take a good look in the mirror, dig out the BS from your past, and face that demon that has been destroying your love life. Love will release value into your life. Love will teach you how to love with a pure heart, not a hurt heart, nor a fearful heart.

    All human beings operate with vibrations in their own body. When we get in-tune with ourselves the universe opens a connection to your soul mate. Your soul mate may or may not be in your life currently, wherever they are he or she will be able to feel your love. The bond and the connection is deepened by your ability to allow love be just what it has been designed to be. The love of a soul mate is so powerful that it reaches beyond your own thoughts and expands higher than your own ways. The love of a soul mate will resemble Gods love for us. This is the purpose of love and relationships -to resemble God's eternal love for us.

    The spirit of God is our guide, our source, and our true bloodline. Thanks to God we will forever be royalty, wealthy, and prosperous. God is forever the apple of my eye. Our love has the ability to grow day after day without ever ending. We are all able to live with an understanding that love does not exist without trust and trust does not exist without love.

"My little children, let us not love in word, neither in tongue; but in deed and in truth."

I John 3:18

about the love goddess

As a woman, you expect to be taught from a male father figure about how to truly love; How you are to receive it, how to live it in, and how to handle things when they are not going the way that you desire for them to go? This is what I grew up thinking. My life lesson was learning how to walk in the essence of love that I saw from watching my Grandparents

while I was younger, but eventually I missed being around their virtue, their strength, and their Godliness. All I was left with were idea's, thoughts, and no real understanding of how to really operate in life with love being the centerpiece.

    I am pretty sure that my parents love one another, but they were not the type to show it due to their military stature. When I was young, there were so many things that I just did not understand and some things I didn't care to understand.

    Questions pondered my mind, my thoughts, even my actions as I contemplated a reason to hold on to this idea of love and the truth of it. Placing my thoughts in God was the only real place for moi, especially when I had not yet learned of my own true identity. What was even worse was that if I met another male that was egotistical with the misconception and idea that to love moi was through him being mean or having an attitude I don't think I could even stand to take it.

Something had to change. I could not for the life of myself understand why the most proud men really believed that strong women liked to be controlled. Or it could have been the fact that my father was not around and the stereotype that females get from men who know that their father was absent in their life? I was stereotyped definitely.

This stupidity was so far from the truth when it came to my life, my love, and my own weaknesses. I have always known deep within myself that I deserve the love of a god {a lower case version of the big guy}. Maybe I thought that love would just appear to moi when I was looking for it or when I least expected, however that was not my case.

My prayer unto God was, *"If you see me, Why would you not just give moi the man in whom you created specifically for moi? I wanted someone that saw moi as the apple of his eye. I wanted to be the love of his life and I wanted you {God} to be his first love?"*

I would know then for sure that I would be his second love next to his first love-

God {the big guy}. I would not even want to be his first. I have experienced that as well. Trust moi when I say that if a man puts you before God, you will soon be bound to hell and damnation. Laughing, however I am so serious! Order means everything!

    A man who will put you first, will eventually hurt you without cause or reason. He won't even know why he is doing it. It will just be a manifestation of him not loving his true god self first. He has to love the God in himself first before he can value the life of the goddess in you.

    I regretted the idea of this book for so many years. It began so many years ago, around 3 am in the morning when I was discovering that there was more to myself, and there was way more to God. The writing process along with life became a huge disappointment to moi over and over again and that is exactly what my life felt like. I was not fooling anyone let alone myself. I wanted to experience what I knew of God in the natural, in the spiritual, and the physical realm of love. I knew that somehow, in some way I was off course when it came to that truth.

I did not want to open myself up to love anymore. I did not want to be hurt by anyone, however the kingdom within moi insisted that there was a greater love for moi to experience here on God's green earth.

A love that would consist of kindness, greatness, trust, pure thoughts, and equality. I knew that if a relationship made moi wake up with the regret of wondering why I ever got in the relationship that maybe it would eventually fail. I had a long journey to travel to come close to gaining understanding of this gift called love.

This is why I wrote this book as an outlet, not an answer. There are so many people striving to be the answer for others when the best thing that you can give another human is love first, your story, and something that will make them question their entire existence. This is what will cause you to look at yourself, you true purpose, and the reason why you are here.

    As I wrote on this book, I freely wrote ideas, titles, thoughts, chapters, books, conclusions, and more conclusions. More books. This book about love seemed to have no end as I began to write about submission, study humanity, study womankind, habits, science, of course God, and human behavior. I did not even know if I was in a real relationship with God. I understood what that would mean of moi so I continued to move forward out of wanting to know, "*Why individuals do certain things, especially things that made no sense with the hope of keeping that person?*" The funniest part to life is when you learn that the individuals who treat you the worse seem to be the ones who are so confident in never losing you. Since we already know that this makes no sense, we will not begin to make sense out of it.

    The by far greatest lesson that I have learned in my journey is that love is not any idea that we could ever imagine, it is not filled with any self-righteous act. Many times I made righteous decisions, but wrong decisions for my life. It is so humanly important to throw out the idea that God is all about righteous choices verses the right choice for our lives. The choices for our lives don't have to make sense to anyone but God and ourselves. When you make a decision to let go of the fear of what you have been taught along with the crazy idea that being righteous would be the only way to be blessed it will make a huge difference in how you live your life. No one is perfect: Remember this! We all have issues and the individuals who are talking the most about everyone else's issues are usually the ones with the most issues. I don't know about you, but I don't have time to be around people who spend most of their time judging the entire world without taking one minute to ever look at their own life. If we all look hard enough there is something that is wrong with each one of us. If we look a tad bit harder there is also something just as great about each one of us. The thing is to start looking at our own greatness so we are able to see and accept the greatness that is in others. Once we examine our own purpose well we can focus whole on being, living, and devoting each of our days to that very purpose.

It is so sad how many of us miss out on love pursuing the idea of it verses the choice to love what is right for you. It did not matter how many times I chose to write and write about it some more, **love was still leading moi** in only one direction, and that was the decision to freely love. Love not only has the will of power, it has the will of freedom.

Welcome to my world of love!

Oh, follow moi on Instagram
@monisoihumes

"every heel that he heard coming down the hallway, he thought it was you
"

—sex in the city

You have to fight for the love that you want just as hard as you are fighting to achieve riches. Make it unconditional.

About Happy Endings

Happy Endings is a book about all the things that try love, with the hope that love is released on the highest level in the lives of each reader. There is no best way to speak on what was meant to be the most awesome part of our lives, our childhood, and our adulthood. in most of our lives when it comes to relationship the word disaster screams loudly all over the planet. Hello! There are so many relationships book out there, but nothing that really stood out for the moi to truly understand that one question, *"How do you have a Happy Ending?"* Laughing, please get your mind out of the gutter. There are many questions that we all ask ourselves, *"How do you reach that certain climax to saying yes that is it, this is the one for moi?"* And if this is the one, then *why does he or she piss moi the fuck off so much?* Sorry Mom and all those who will never verbally hear moi say a word such as Fuck in their presence. If you are reading this and dislike the profanity there is a {Godly Version} available online. The truth is that I have issues, but I am pretty sure that you know that already about moi since you have watched my life over the years. Yes I have problems, but love is not one of them. It just seems that way from a distance.

What excites moi the most about this book is very important. The mere fact that I have learned that throughout the entire process that we are all in control of our ending whether good or bad. What we face today is a reflection of what we believed to be true the day before. Sorry to burst anyone's bubble, but this is the part where you all by your lonesome become accountable for what you are about to encounter as you read this awesome book titled **"Happy Endings."** As you prepare to read about my own life, the parts that sucked liked hell, the craziest shit that you would never think would ever have happened to someone like moi. This is also the part where you accept that we are all some peculiar ass people, each and every last one of us are so fucking unique. I apologize Mom. But you were warned. I am going to say a lot of fucking shit that you might not want to hear, but I am 100% sure that you have heard worse since we live in a fucking world that is filled with horrendous abominations. That is why it is so important for us all to love again, for us to show the children that love is still in our hearts, to show young men how to love as men, and to show young girls the respect and value of love. If we take a look at the children who are following the footsteps of the ways of this world, then we will have to also take a look at ourselves.

  Many times it has been told to moi that I would be a preacher, and that I would help people to live the lives that they were purposed to lived. This is my passion but my delivery is different.

I discovered that the world is already filled with preachers everywhere. Ok. Literally and they are having such a hard time, because everyone ridicules them for saying Fuck, having sex, drinking a glass of red wine (come on you have to be kidding moi. I could not do this), buying jets, having affairs, desiring great financial futures, and not too mention what is said of them when they desire to have a little fun {T.D. Jakes}. I am in no way speaking bad against any of these Pastors, I am simply stating the fact that the world has literally talked about them for being human beings + pastors.

On this journey I have learned that none of us are perfect and if we are going to help anyone is this life that we are living we must first start with the fact that we are all fucked up in our own little way. There is nothing perfect about moi. I wish, but nah I will take this eventual life that I have and learn it all over again if it helps moi to be who I really am.

In reality, we are all little girls inside the adult bodies of women who desires who still desire to have a fairy tale ending, a happy ending, an ending filled with love, companionship, romance, life, adventure, fun, and spur of the moment shit; like the shit you don't plan for. It just makes your day all worth while. Yes I am and will remain a hopeful romantic at heart.

If anyone wants to take any shots at moi, go right ahead just remember that I said it first that my life has been fucked up just like everyone else's. Although we spend so much time gossiping about people like Kim Kardashians, calling her a whore, or saying that she is fake. Love you chick. I love their show. Period! Keep doing you. What makes her any different than any of us? We all have been smashing (having sex), some are just better off at hiding it than others. Men stop dissing women for what is natural, especially since you are the ones in whom females are having sex with. Sex is just apart of life. There has been so much time spent on downing females for doing the same things that men are doing with them and it makes no sense. If you have an issue with women then stop supporting half naked females on Facebook, stop sending direct messages to females with their ass as their profile pics. What I am saying is that it is easy to talk about a problem verses being apart of fixing the problem.

    The media has just made it easier for us to focus on the lives of others rather than focus on the fact that our lives are just as fucked as the people that we are watching, they just made it to the big screen with their life. These people are bold, courageous, invigorating, and people all over the world admire the shit out of them because they went after what they love even if it meant you watching them under a telescope as you judge every move that they make. By the way I think that Kim Kardashian is awesome if you really study her life and what she has been through a lot when it has came to matters of the heart. Kim is one of the most judged females on tv. She cannot even gain weight without the media taking it and running 10 miles with it the information.

When she started her career she began her own E-bay business {Kim sold her belongings to survive on her own}, and started a closet (organizing) business. Paris Hilton use to be one of her clients before she began to be noticed by paparazzi herself. The sad thing is that all everyone remembers of her is the fact that she had sex tape with Ray'J. Sex is all that majority of this world ever notices. My point is stop judging everyone and if you want to be biblical about it, then it has been said, *"Judge and you shall be judged."*

We are all just human beings living life, even if it is for that one moment, it is both the desire of male and female to reach a **happy ending.**

And sometimes that takes time to reach.

words to know while reading

energy
has the ability to transform into another form, the total amount of physical and mental strength to do something

God
:*the big guy*

god
:*a lower case version of the big guy*

goddess
:*a lower case female version of the big guy*

Ka' {*Egyptian*} and Chi {*Chinese*}
:*a spiritual energy*

Love
:*God, the heart*

The Godly Version
:clean

Pastors
:human beings who have the same problems as everyone else, however they are called to a higher level and expected to walk in obedience without spot or blemish

Meditation
:a form of breathing, also increases your sexual energy

Moi
:me

Nadis
:channel in which life force energy (prana) circulates

Samadhi *{Hindu}*
:A heightened state of awareness, an intense concentration accomplished through meditation: a final stage at which union with the divine is reached; you are able to feel power

Sound mind
:a mind that is a rest life and it lives and breathes through clarity

Tantric Sex
: where the two are exchanging masculine and feminine energy are transmitting this energy between the two bodies. It can last for hours, there is no thought of it ending, it is more spiritual than sexual.

Thirst
:the desire to be needed verses the desire to be wanted

Trust
:The breath of love

Vibrations:
when slight movement occurs that creates a direct result

Introduction to *Happy Endings*

In the world that we live in all marketers understand something that even everyday people seem to lack, they have this uncanny ability to connect to human emotions. This is what any relationship is, having the ability to connect with someone outside of yourself. When a relationship lacks this link it is hard to make it last without the feeling of something being missing. It takes effortless energy to connect to another human being. All you have to do is open up and just feel, take a deep breathe, and feel some more. This is also a form of meditation.

Everything that we do, how we act, how we live, and how we chose to love our partner is all a reflection of how we feel on the inside. Having massive amounts of love for yourself gives you the capability to have massive amounts of love for your partner.

Life and love grabs your attention best when you focus on it. As you tune in and tune out the noise you will again feel the spirit of peace that rests in the spirit of a sound mind. Love is and always will be the greatest gift given unto mankind {human race}. Love opens up doors that no man can close, this is why more that anything it is fought tooth and nail. There is a negative entity that is pulling to suck the life out of you and your partner living in the truth of love.

Are there any boundaries that exist?

There really aren't any, if there were, lets just say we would all be living by them. Right? If you knew that there was something that you could do, boundaries that you could set that would change your love life forever you would live by them right? We all would. Then again I think that was supposed to be the Bible and we are not doing so great at that now are we? There are so many things that are in place and the truth is the only thing that it has done is set boundaries on all of us loving one another. There are so many other things that we see such as clothing, symbols, culture, skin color, race, religion, politics, and social status. All this things that we are looking at stand before we ever attempt to look at the love first. Boundaries is the reason why it takes so much for some of us to be successful at love, life, and relationships.

Then of course there are the small few who have hardly any boundaries and they are usually the ones who are really successful in their careers yet lacking in love. These individuals sacrifice having a personal life for their career. This is another thing that many individuals were taught that they could have a successful career if they sacrificed having a personal life.

Then there are the rebels. The rebels want it all. You could draw a line right in front of a rebel and that same rebel would cross that same line every time. Why? Rebels hate to feel like you are cutting their cord from freedom. Rebels love freely. Rebels walk, run, and breathe to the beat of their own heart. They are risk takers, investors in business and life. Their gut instincts tell them to fuck everyday normal living and to pursue their dreams. They walk in the fullness of their own power and they tell fear to go fuck off.

We are all classified into groups, categories, and personalities; this is how we all became so picky that we don't even know how to follow the spirit that is within us anymore. We prefer to live on the outside of life instead of in it.

The funny thing is that we live in a world where growing up with the fairy tale idea of love and happiness is the ultimate goal and when you get a dose of life, love becomes hate to some. This is the goal of any negative entity, to turn your desire from love into hatred.

If your thoughts, feelings, and actions cause you to hate love, if it keeps you from becoming love, and being in love there is something wrong with that picture. As God has intended that when it is all said and done that you will and shall have love for all of man kind even as the spirit holds, possess, and breathes love for each being that walks the face of this earth.

The spirit is so powerful that it has placed over 7 billion people in a world and by the second the number literally continues to increase, that is over 300,000 births a day, over 100,000 deaths a day, and population growth of over 200,000 a day, and over 44 million population growth, and by the time that you read this number will have increased.[1]

China is the number 1 fastest growing population with over 1.4 billion in population. This really amazed my mind, because for the past 30 years China has had

---

[1] m.worldmeters.info/world-population/

a one child policy. Apparently when they have child number two the government starts giving out bonuses. This just goes to show again that when you set boundaries no one listens. If China did listen then it would be the slowest growing population not the fastest. [2]

When the right energy connects they can't stay away from each other, they continue to grow, multiply, and populate the world. This is why this book holds so much value, because why put stipulations on love, life, living, and giving birth? Love is real freedom.

Love is kind. Love is polite. Love is freedom. Love is who we are and if we allow anyone or anything to change that or to cause us to give up on this gift we are just letting ourselves down in the long run.

After struggling with love and relationships for the longest, it still did not dawn on my moi that there was something inside of moi that was way bigger than my own understanding. I had to realize that there are just as many people addicted to love as they are money. Welcome to my world with the chaos that I experienced, plus some delightful insight.

Chapter 1
ASHLEY MADISON EFFECT

There has been so much commotion in the year of 2015 about the Ashley Madison ordeal, so many men, powerful, married men were found guilty for having accounts on this website. The website has over 41 Million anonymous members who are subscribed to the website.

The sites tag line is:

Life is short. Have an affair.

When it went viral there were so many husbands who were on the website and everyone was shocked to find out the site was hacked releasing the names of some of those men who were in the public's eye. Another thing that you noticed is that the site says, *"It's easy."* Men work all the time, they want and need to come home to an easy atmosphere. AshleyMadison.com understands that there was a huge market for this and went for it. 80% of men cheat for sex. The site is owned by Avid Dating Life or Avid Life Media. The company also owns other brands:

CougarLife.com
Establishedmen.com

This company has found a need and created a solution for many individuals with {male and female} problems. They are able to provide a service simply from understanding their own target market. Everyone from all over the universe wants and desires to be wanted, not necessarily needed. There is a difference between being needed (thirst) and being wanted. In relationships we have to remember that a huge part of having our partners is the fact that we showed a desire for them, this is what drew them in. We all want to be desired at the end of each day. Desire is the very thing that excites a man to come home to you. Desire is the very thing that excites a woman to feel almost like a little girl waiting for him to come home to her. This is what

> "Desire cannot be missing from the relationship."
>
> *#lovewins*

Ashleymadison.com created through their brand, they created a way to capture the hearts of man and fill a desire that they knew men desired to be pleased.

    I am not saying that it is right, nor am I saying that it is wrong. I am just saying that we all have desires that we all will make sure that are met. As upsetting as this may have been to all those wives who thought that they had committed husbands. These men still had a need in which they obviously felt like was not being fulfilled at home. Although this is something that we hate to admit, but sexual intercourse plays a major role in relationships. Men are sexual beings, this is how they show that they are attracted to you ladies. I am not saying that it is all that a man wants, but sex to men is like communication to women. Both counterparts want something and when it is not given sometimes it causes the other person to look elsewhere. In this situation it has caused men to look outside of their relationship to find sexual fulfillment. When men come home, they want to come home to a peaceful place, a sanctuary, they want to be pleased, they want to eat, and they want you to forget about how long and hard your day was and give in to the pleasure. It is that simple.

 Sometimes ladies make this so hard, we want men to understand how hard our day is, when they have had just as hard of day themselves. We often easily fall into the role of selfishness with the ME, ME, ME attitude. It is all about ME syndrome. It is about us. You have to let go of the me for the us. You have to learn to let go and mature enough to be the woman who respects her man, and the little girl at heart who will always cherish his love. This is so valuable to your love, your life, and your relationship. It may not make sense right now, however that is only because you are still holding on to the me instead of the us.

If you do not get this right then you must also accept the fact that if your man is not strong enough to want to keep waiting for you to want and desire him that you are allowing anyone to come in and become a side chick. Although men care nothing about a side chick they truly would prefer to be fulfilled by their woman. Know this. Of course there are some men who are just jerks and they are the exception, however if you have a man that loves and desires you make sure that you keep him happy before he starts wandering around.

It is a set up for you later to act like you didn't know that he was not happy, and for you to get upset with him when you find out he is cheating. Also stop using your vagina to control him that never works, never. You are only under the illusion that it is working. Real men know that they can get sex from anywhere, they desire to be desired. This is more than just sex.

"A man should not go a day without your good loving if he wants it."

A man should not go a day without your good loving if he wants it. You should be putting it on your man whenever he wants to have sex. Remember that energy sometimes changes with age, it increases more in women the older that they get, it decreases in some men the older they get. Gods and goddess are way different when it comes to their sexual energy for the two of them love pleasure. The two of them have a high attraction to one another. When you have a god with great energy, you need to put on your crown and fulfill his desires. When you have a goddess with great energy you need to fulfill her desires.

Make sex apart of your marriage, your relationship, and make it apart of pleasing your man. He has a desire, make sure that you are the one to fulfill it. Don't leave room for another woman to come in and do what you have the power and capabilities to do yourself. Don't just settle with having the man, the home, and the bacon to cook up. Give your man the goods, because he has given you half of everything. He chose you to be his prize, his goddess, his trophy, his Queen, his wife, his boo, his Bae, and his lady. The greatest thing that you can do is show him constantly that you appreciate and value him for every ounce of the hard work that it took for him to be a better man for himself and a better man for you.

    Don't risk losing your treasure by giving him away to trash. Treasure him, he chose you to be in the castle with him. He gave you access to live a fruitful life, show him that he has been given favor from the universe, from God by being with you. Show him that there will be nothing but more blessings from the two of you connecting, uniting, and bonding. Show him that you will keep praying, meditating, and focusing on his increase.

A woman who understands her power in having positive thinking will not lose. It is your responsibility to keep your thoughts positive. It is not his job to do this for you. It is not his job to hear a bunch of problems when he comes home. It is not his job to be punished for your bad day. If he can forget about his hard day then so can you. Stop begin selfish, start loving him, or stop wasting his time, and making him feel guilty for finding another woman to do what you refuse to. Life is tough for everyone, suck it up. Shut up and love him like you desire to be loved! You have it made, because in the world that we live in if you have a man that loves you, works hard, and comes home to you then you definitely have it made. Have you ever heard the saying, *"A piece of a man is better than not having a man."* All men will give you a piece of them and it is up to to fit the position of being his better half. Together the two of you form one whole, solid bond. Stop tripping.

I wanted to specifically point this out because a huge number of the male population is subscribed to the AshleyMadison website, which is available in many different languages in just about every country. It is easy for a man to access another woman just as quick as you nag him, give him an attitude, and constantly tell him no to sex. When a man hears no, he hears the fact that you are rejecting him, you are not desiring him, and that is all he hears.

We must realize that we all hold the key and power to live a happy life, but if we are not happy we cannot expect a man to fix that for us it is only a problem from within oneself.

To all the ladies who feel like they have their man on lock because he is just quiet while you are speaking. The only reason he is quiet is because he is tired of hearing your damn mouth. He cannot wait until you shut up! He may not be cheating, but he definitely is not in a hurry to get home to you either. It does not matter what type of man that you have, know that no man cares to have a woman who feels like she is better at wearing the pants than him. You need to make sure that when and if you raise sand with him that it is a very important reason. Pick and chose your battles wisely.

    A man should not have to deal with his woman having a bad attitude every single week. If you are doing this to him every week, then you should really be ashamed of yourself. Start respecting him and being his hearts desire. Remember Bitches are waiting for you to fuck up.

Chapter 2
LOVE + SEX

> "If you become meditative while making love, the quality of sex changes, and something new enters into it – it becomes tantric, it becomes prayerful, it becomes meditative, it becomes Samadhi."
>
> – *Osho*

Although some couples hate to admit that sex is a problem in their relationships. If you are not having sexual intercourse it can become a huge issue. I have heard different stories about this issue from a man's perspective and a woman's. The fact that we both mature sexually at different ages in our lives does not help things either. Men usually hit their prime in their older teens and early 20's whereas woman hit their prime in their late 30's. This is when women are sexually driven, their hormones are often through the roof while most men hormones calm down. Unless you have been blessed with a guy with high energy levels. This will make for a great love life between the two of you, especially if you are matching in energy.

    Then there are other outside forces that are also a real life issue- porn. There are so many people addicted to porn. The numbers are just crazy. This is an interruption in the sex lives of many couples. Men and women are watching porn by the second right now as you are reading this.

According to Huffington Post 70% of men are watching porn, while 30% of women are watching porn. The average time visitors are spending on porn site is a total of 12 minutes per visit. There is no wonder it is so hard to stay focused on your relationship alone. Sex is everywhere and thanks to the internet it is easy to access. The problem is that not enough individuals are spending time working on putting that same energy into their own partners.

As a woman who meditates and prays I have found that every time that you log online, partake in something such as different activities they all require for you to release energy from within yourself. I am not sure if relationships are struggling just because couples don't care anymore or if there is just a lack of knowledge where energy is concerned.

We all are vibrating at different frequencies, our energy is all operating on different wave lengths. There are multiple ways that we can build and increase our sexual energy between our relationships through simple practices that we are normally not even thinking about as we go about our day.

1. Eat with your partner {Energy is in your food}
2. Meditate together {Energy flows through meditation. When we meditate we activate the **Kundalini** energy which is great for sex in addition to living a successful life}
3. Pray with your partner {Prayers produces energy}
4. Build and work on a project with your partner {Release productive energy}
5. Have fun with your partner {More happy energy releases}

When we understand that energy is everywhere we begin to focus on where we place our energy. Energy is in music and the things that we listen to. Energy is transmitted through tv, reality shows, movies, and the people who we are around.

This is why certain groups do not allow outsiders to come in, they are working to keep the energy within that group on the same frequency. If partners would focus on this and the power that we hold through our energy we will have greater sex lives + greater sex. Sex is energy that we are able to share with our partner.

Yogic wisdom states that there are 72,000 energy channels, called nadis, in the energetic body, and that out of this vast number there are three main channels that direct the primary flow of energy through the body.

There are many forms of energy that are flowing through our bodies. Ka' {Egyptian} and Chi {Chinese} is a spiritual energy that is in our bodies that is activated through breathing techniques. This helps with our spiritual energy.

I am not trying to prove that we are all the same, however in reality we are all the same and what makes us different is the energy that we take in and the levels of it in which we operate on. What you want to do is begin to focus on being in a state of meditation while having sex, desiring nothing but being in the moment in which you are in. This is **tantric sex** *where the two are exchanging masculine and feminine energy are transmitting this energy between the two bodies. It can last for hours, there is no thought of it ending, it is more spiritual than sexual.* This release will come with increased pleasure. There is not much pleasure when you are operating only in the physical realm of sexual intercourse, this is why it can get boring for some verses it being pleasurable each time you are sexually involved with your mate.

You will want to awaken yourself to this energy that is within you. It should become a goal to unlock the magic. It works even if only one of you operate in this magical energy, however if the two of you do it then the energy increases together. It makes it feel magical to both partners during sexual intercourse.

"The universe is a web of energy conveying life force"

I decided to do some online research only to find that so many couples have complaints when it comes to their sex life. When couples know that they are facing an issue their first priority is to fix the problem before it gets worse. In reality couples do not seek help until it is worse. Until you have reach that point of saying verbally, "I can't stand that mf." Once this is released from your mouth so is all the negative energy that comes along with the statement itself. A wise woman once told moi that the best way to solve any problem is to get to the root of the actual problem itself.

I was online reading an article on Huffington Post by Brittany Wong title, *"10 Complaints Sex Therapists Hear All the Time," Plus the advice they give couples in their offices.* I found this article to be very interesting.

The article covered actual problems that are reported to different sex therapists about sex and relationships. There were a total of seven sex therapist and psychologists from around the country who agreed to share problems from different couples. This was very interesting.

Both men and women in relationships usually have totally separate issues when it comes to relationships when add sex to that well either she wants it or he doesn't, or he wants and she does not. It has become rare that two individuals in a relationship are on the same page when it comes to their sex life. I am not saying it does not happen, but very often it happens at different times. On the other hand when couples first begin to have sex it is usually really great in the beginning then they eventually get bored or the honeymoon phase of sex dies down for whatever reason or excuse that is created for the reason as to why.

 Relationships only fail because individuals fail to do what they did in the beginning. Individuals get comfortable and forget about the pleasure that sex offers the both of them. They get caught up in life, work, kids, family problems, and bills which all have nothing to do with their sex life at all.

 From the article I chose to quote these following quotes, because it shows an example of the female and the male view on their sex life and relationship.

"Women who come into my office often tell me they wish they could climax the 'real' way -- through intercourse. The clitoris, however, *not* the vagina is the center of her sexual and pleasure nerve endings. In fact, only about 15-20 percent of all women can climax during sexual intercourse and even then she needs lots of vibration, manual or oral stimulation to get her close. For those who still want to try likely positions, I recommend two with good G-spot-penile contact: Either woman-on-top at a 45 degree angle, or woman-lying-on-her-back on a relatively firm surface with her hips rocked up (for instance, with her knees hooked around his elbows)." -- *Laurie Watson, LMFT, certified sex therapist*

"I frequently see couples where the man is confused about why he doesn't want to have sex and the woman is the frustrated one. Without a clear answer, I end up asking a ton of questions trying to decipher why. If it's

because he feels too dependent or too close to his partner, distancing is the goal. Most commonly, men complain to me about not getting the loving contact they want. He may feel she goes through the motions, treats sex like a chore, or just lies there when he wants more love, contact, emotion and presence. Women sometimes make the mistake of thinking their partners are just trying to satisfy a biological need and treat sex in a perfunctory manner, to 'please' the guy. But this shuts men down; they want more passion than that. I remind couples that passion requires engagement, expression, eye contact and trying to really *feel*. It's more than touch."
-- *Brandy Engler, Ph.D and author of The Women on My Couch*

Men and women both have a desire to be satisfied, sometimes they just do not know how to get on the same page when it comes to the importance of allowing sex to be a free space in their relationship verses an actual obligation. When you feel obligated to do something it makes it hard for you to do it all.

Passion does not need to be told or asked for, it is done out of mere love. Couples have forgotten the importance and value of loving one another.

A great sex life is all part of having a healthy monogamous relationship, without a great sex life the two of you suffer emotionally, mentally, and physically. It should be your goal to please your partner and to find out what that means to them, because there are so many other outside sources looking to grab his / her attention with porn being one of those things, strippers, daily TV advertisements, billboards, Facebook, Instagram, and the list goes on. The point is that there are so many things that are working to interrupt your relationship.

If you desire to increase your sex life between you and your partner there are things that the two of you can do to increase that energy between you.

1. Pray
2. Meditate {practice your breathing, it will increase the feeling, and the pleasure}
3. Yoga
4. Eating healthy. You body has to be involved. The healthier you are the better.
5. Drink plenty H2O
6. Speak in your desire towards one another
7. Flirt, plenty of flirting
8. Spend time alone to yourself growing who you are. You can do this even if the two of you live together.

In conclusion to this chapter, there are several things that we can do to increase our sex lives with our partner. We must be wiling to step out of our comfort zones to listen and to try new things. We must look at our sex life with our partner as an opportunity to grow closer in bond. Many issues and complaints can arise from having poor sex lives with our partners and we are the only ones who can get a handle on improving this. Enjoy having tantric sex, activate the kundalini energy that is in you body now. Take a 20 minute break from reading and just meditate. Focus on activating this energy in your body, allow it to travel up your spine, and release worry, frustration, doubt, and fear completely from your mind, body, and soul right now. There is a level of happiness within your body waiting on you to just release it.

Chapter 3

STOP QUALIFYING BOTTOM BITCHES

The damn things we hear men say are crazy. What? Bottom bitches? Really? What? What? What? Ok since we know they are out there, stop qualifying bottom bitches to be even considered as a qualifying component that will potentially destroy your relationship. She should not even be in the mix nor an option. Period! There are way too many females competing with bottom chicks + side chicks which = a disaster, any way that you look at it. If you feel like your lady is not enough then why are you with her? This is crazy! It is completely outraging seeing how many females who are on Facebook going to war with another female who is also screwing her man. Ladies when you allow this, a man will keep doing it to you. My opinion if you are the one that is accepting other females begin on the side, you may be the bottom bitch. You may be the one who has no self esteem, self respect, nor true confidence in yourself. Or you just may want to have your cake while keeping your freedom. There are reasons for everything and that is understanding, however at some point you have to think about everyone that is involved especially if you are noticing that the man is not caring. We have to become accountable to stick together to make sure that relationships and families are surviving.

We play a role in this as well. Men at the same time stop giving the hoes attention when you know full and well that if your lady ever stepped out on you that you would not be able to handle it. We all need to be cautious of the karma that we are releasing into the universe so that it does not bite us in the ass.

Anytime a women excuses a man in doing whatever he wants just off of the strength of him being a man, there is a problem with that. There is no man worth losing your own worth over. By allowing him to do something that puts your relationship in jeopardy, because you feel like that is what men do is no excuse for you allowing it. All women and all men treat relationships according to how they have been treated, they view their partners based on how a man or women has previously treated them. I am not saying all do this, but most do this. It takes a real woman or a real man to admit that the way that you have done things in the past didn't work, because they didn't work at the relationship. Stop trying to carry dead habits into a new relationship. If every man has cheated on you and you have thought that every man will cheap on you then it is time that you stop thinking like that. As a man think so is he, therefore let it go. If it has not worked, it is not going to until you form new thinking habits. You have been the same denominator in all of your relationships, you have something to do with how they began and how they ended. Stop lying to yourself first, no one is in a relationship alone, and no one destroys a relationship alone. My experience is that men are generally some of the most faithful creatures that God has created, I will keep thinking this. Your thoughts are powerful.

    Now what I needed to work on was the fact at one point in my life I thought that I only attract a guy who would be madly in love with moi, but did not know how to treat moi. I overcame this thought, this is when meditation came into full effect into my life. **Goodbye thought, for you are only a memory of my distant past. You are no longer related to my future. Deuces! In fact, middle finger up! IJS! I am glad that you are only a memory of what is behind moi and you have absolutely nothing to do with what is in front of moi.**

Life goes on, so do people. If someone does not know how to treat you, do not be afraid to give their ass the boot. Bye! Lets make something clear we are not speaking on letting someone out of your life over something minor. A couple can survive some really tough shit, but we must make sure that we are doing the right thing by our relationship.

If a man has a side bitch + a bottom bitch, which one are you? What category do you think that your man has put you in? Are you a goddess? Men place women into categories when they first meet them. I grew up with nothing but brothers + I have many other brothers {Thanks Dad, aka Rolling Stone} so all of what I know of men came from listening to them and watching them behave. They categorize us ladies. Their categories consist of:

    1. Hoe
    2. Side Bitch
    3. Bottom Bitch {Same as a hoe. He has no care, nor concern for her at all. She has no value.}
    4. Bitch
    5. Friend
    6. Lady
    7. Queen
    8. Goddess

When a man meets his goddess, side bitch + bottom bitch + plus his girl, all of them take an exit out of his life! When a man falls in love, he is not focused on holding on to dead situations. A man if he knows nothing else, he knows when he has found a good thing. A goddess is his good thing.

A side bitch is not hoe in a man's mind. She is comfort when needed. She is just someone that is there when he needs her, but he does not want her as a permanent situation. Side bitches want the position of a goddess, but most guys remain not interested in giving her this position. Please note that a man can be in a serious relationship and still have a side bitch. Just because you are a wife does not mean you are a goddess.

A bottom bitch is border line trash, a man has no respect for her at all. Please note that I heard this from the mouth of a man. I asked him how men view the women in their life. She is just a way for him to release himself and keep it moving.

If you are his lady or his girl start practicing reaching goddess level. If not side bitches can easily get in the picture.

Now a goddess she can hold her own, she is comfort to him when he needs it. She is a friend, a partner, a cook, a cleaner, a cheerleader, and she gives up the goods whenever her man needs or wants it. She does not hold back her love from him ever. She makes his dreams come true. She prays for him. She is his cheerleader. She waits for him to come home with open arms. She is not quick to nag him. She withholds nothing good from her man. She knows how to budget, grind, build, save, teach, and keep.

Now that you understand this, why would a man who has found this need any other woman? Go through this carefully. ATTENTION! IF YOU ARE DOING ALL OF THE ABOVE THERE IS NO NEED FOR YOU EVER TO WORRY ABOUT YOUR MAN HAVING ANYONE ELSE! PERIOD!

I don't believe that two people have to get married in front of a judge in order for them to be destined to be together for ever.

Keep and maintain as much control over your life as possible. Know that you are only bound by the thoughts that you think and know to be true for yourself.

Ride or die means that no matter what the two of you face together that loyalty and faithfulness will remain between the two of you. Stop explaining this to people and using it as an excuse for you {male or female} to have other partners, that is not what it means.

When you fall in love and reach a level of maturity, you should be done with the BS. At some point if you want something worth having, you will need to give up something. Sacrifice is essential when it comes to gaining in life. You cannot have and keep a treasure holding on to trash.

Ladies stop giving the goods to the wrong men. Men stop giving the goods to the wrong women. Everyone at some point has done so, just admit it to yourself, and keep it moving. At the end of the day you live, breath, and consume what you chose to. Chose wisely!

> **"Shout out to all the Boss bitches wifing niccas."**

In the words of Drake, *"Shout out to all the Boss bitches wifing niccas."* Huh! What? Yea, but it happens everyday. *Make sure that you hit him with a prenup, tell that man to ease up.* I laughed hard ass hell when I heard this song when Drake came out with it. Ladies we all know that we have been with an ignorant ass man that did not deserve the time or day, but they run a good ass game on you. No thanks I will pass!

A smart woman, a smart man does not want nor desire a relationship with an ignorant ass person. You can kick rocks with that. Again, bye, and deuces! Be with someone who loves and adores you enough to weather through any storm with you. Know their heart, and the intent of their heart. Once you know the intent of their heart, this will make it easier for you to face adversity any time it wants to hit the two of you in the face. Stick it out! Love on each other as much as possible, there is a reason why the two of you are together!

Chapter 4

LADIES LET'S GIVE OUR GUYS WHAT THEY WANT

Ladies if you want a real man then it will also require you being a real woman. We go through life thinking that our way is the only way, however if you remember that Queens are the most powerful piece on the board of chess, and all Kings know this. He will not release his power unless he knows that the Queen in which he chooses can handle the power that he gives her. This means that you must be prepared for him before you even meet him.

Women are often very strong willed. We feel that we know everything and many times we know a lot, however we must learn that if we want a relationship to be successful that we have to back down and give our men what they want. We are all taught that a happy woman, a happy home. I believe as well that a happy man, will produce a happy woman. The two of them work hand in hand. There are way too many homes where the woman is happy and the man is not. There are also way too many homes where the man is happy and the woman is not. The goal to having a truly happy home is balance.

In creating balance again we must first get to the root of our issues. This is where we must begin, especially if we desire to have a happy ending.

A man will respond to a woman's greatness as well as their foolishness. Make sure that you are wise in which one that you want to him to respond to. It is your life not mine.

Ladies: The best thing that you can do is back down from all manners of the following:

1. Selfishness
2. Bad attitudes {This will get you kicked to the curve, when you think about it there is no success that comes with negative energy so don't think that you can have a successful

relationship with a your guy if you don't know how to talk to him or treat him as the King or god that he is}

3. The power of the pussy. We have heard this saying for centuries. The question is, *"Are you doing it right?"* Maybe not. Trying to run your guy with your vagina. {Men love to have sex, but if you think that you are going to tell him what to do just because you are giving it up the 'p' then you are sadly mistaken}

4. Too Spoiled! If you are spoiled and you have attracted him then your guy probably loves the fact that you are spoiled. He even desires to spoil you. He looks at this like you are not just going for anything. It turns him on, but don't be a bitch about

don't be a bitch about it.

it. {He loves the fact that you have some standards and that you want your way, but don't take that shit to the extreme}

5. Needy {Men dislike it when you are too needy} Slow that shit down. Keep it to a minimum. Know when to and when not to act this way. Behave accordingly.

6. Accusations {Men hate when you are constantly accusing them of things, if you are having bad vibes, check your own emotions first; it just may be coming from bad experiences in your past relationships and you are carrying those feelings into what could be a great relationship}

7. Stop being a side chick; you are getting in between someone's relationship. You are also sewing a bad seed in your own life. Step it up to first class.

As females we spend so much time applying pressure to our guy to make them grow up that sometimes we forget to deal with ourselves. If we take a good look in the mirror it could change a lot for a good relationship. Men are not the only ones who could use a little growing up, us women could benefit from growing up a tad bit ourselves. Stop feeling like the man is the only one who needs to look in the mirror! Females have just as many issues.

    As a woman I knew that I was spoiled, but being a spoiled brat in a relationship will eventually get you no where. A man will get tired of that shit. Don't get moi wrong being spoiled is cute to a man, but only to a certain degree. You need to know how to turn your spoiled ass down a notch before your being spoiled ass begins to sound like a radio of nagging. It is all the same to him. If you are asking him for too much, you are telling him that he is not doing enough. If you are straight out nagging him, you are not caring that you are telling him that he is not doing enough.

Men want simplicity, give them a little patience + respect and they are good. Stop overdoing it! Give him the time to work things out, he is working in God's time not woman's time. By understanding this, you are the one who saves time. Don't make things harder on yourself, trust moi when you make it harder on him you are only making it harder on yourself in return.

Why you are out buying up everything, see if there is some wisdom for sale while you are out blowing money. Listen this is not for every women, this is for every woman that are in those same shoes that I have been in before. Let moi save you the heartache. We do not all have to go through the heart ache, some things we can look, learn, and listen from others. This is important especially if you want a long term relationship.

Another thing about a great guy is he will invite you out everywhere he goes when he feels that you are down with him. He enjoys sharing his time with you, however this is not your open door to take advantage of his time all the time. Back off and give him the space to enjoy the guy things with his friends. Trust moi when I say that he will appreciate you for it each time that you give him the respect that he deserves and understanding. If you do everything with him all you are doing is setting yourself up for him to regret you.

When your guy is hanging with the guys, take some time to enjoy the quiet time, eat some ice cream, work on your business, watch a movie, take a hot shower, or do your hair. Your guy is coming back home and when he does he will be more than ready to give it to you, because there is nothing more sexy than a man coming home to his confident woman who is not giving him a hard time just for being a guy.

It is ok to go out with him and his friends sometimes, especially if he is insisting on you going to a game or even a party with him just know when you need to back off. He doesn't invite the guys when he is spending alone time with you, "Does he?" No he doesn't, because he respects and values his time alone with you and you need to respect and value his time alone with his friends. Men need their time to talk, scream, and curse without worrying about if they are offending you or not. There is no need to shoot yourself in the foot, your guy's friends will appreciate you for this as well.

Send your man away with a peace of mind that his lady loves and trust him to do just what he said he is going to do. Most men are faithful when they have found a woman that they truly love. This is something you can hold dear to your heart.

A man will stay away from a woman that does not trust him. Give him trust and he will love the shit out of you. Serious! He will come home and rock your world every night. :)

Chapter 5
LOVE IS PERFECTED THROUGH PATIENCE!

Love is such a precious, loving, and awesome gift, and human beings everywhere want a piece of it. The questions is how do we get the chance or the opportunity to share this awesome gift with another human being, especially after being hurt so many times? This is very important to the success of your relationship, because before we can truly look at someone we must learn to have enough patience to love ourselves. When you are in love with who you are, you will attract a partner that loves who they are. We spend so much time blaming others for hurting and saying that we need to just kick people out of our lives. The thing is, I am not sure how many of us take a good look in the mirror at ourselves. A self realization is life changing.

You cannot love anyone until you take the time to learn to love you. This process for some can be a small amount of time, for some it could be years, for some longer than that; it just depends on that individual and their own personal needs. Relationships are meant to bring joy to one another. When you see two individuals who are happy and in love with one another 9 times out of 10 they are also in love with who they are. Love gives love. Hurt gives hurt. We give what we know, who we are, and how we are.

There are also those times in which we are in situations where we are showing someone what love is through us loving them, through the act of being kind, and when we exercise being patient. When you are patient and kind to others who are mean and angry they will eventually wonder why. This is not to say that you must make it a habit to be around these types of people, this is to say that we all have had our season where patience has come through us in the form of love to show others that the love of God is very real. This is why love is bound to win.

    Hurt individuals will continue to cry wolf until they get tired of it, this is why we must draw a line between loving them and trying to pull them out of something. You cannot pull anyone out of anything, this must be a personal decision that is made by that person themselves. When they are ready for change, when you are ready for change you will find yourself being exactly where you need to be and when you need to be there.

I remember this day in which I was sitting at the house by myself, I could feel this tug on the inside of my spirit. I wanted to do something, however I was unsure of what that something was so I just meditated. Once I finished, I got in the shower, got dressed, and headed downtown, Atlanta to a coffee shop. When I walked inside I noticed a group of individuals there. I walked passed them and could feel great energy within my spirit that was connecting moi to them. I still had a seat on the other side of the coffee shop by the window. I asked one of the guys who worked there if he knew what the meeting was about. He was kind of unsure but he said, *"It is like a church, but it is not a church."*

I responded, "Well is it ok for moi to go over there? Or is it just for them?" I wanted to know if it was exclusive before I just walked over. But anyway.

The dude said, "*No I think that it is for anyone.*"

I responded, "*Cool.*" And if you know moi then you know that I got up with no hesitation.

I got my things, and went to have a seat right there in their circle. It was that easy. The leader introduced himself, "*Hi, I am Judah. Who invited you out tonight?*"

I responded, "*No one. I could feel how great the energy was over here, before I got here I was meditating, and knew that it was time to do something different. I just flowed with the energy.*"

Judah responded, "*Awesome, that is awesome. Well we are glad that you are here.*" Judah is now one of the cast members of Preachers of Atlanta.

You see I was ready for change. I was ready to love myself on a new level. I was ready to connect with new people. I was ready to live a new and improved lifestyle. And all because I was ready, the universe and God presented the moment of opportunity right there for moi. All I had to do in order to receive this opportunity was have a seat. Life can be this simple when you are ready to love. Life connected moi with an awesome group of individuals who all have self love for themselves and love for one another. I was able to receive this love through having patience and through lacking fear.

Spirituals connections only take place when you remove fear out of the way. Love has to be present. The more you learn and get to know what love is, the more that love in you will be perfected. You will begin to perfect yourself instead of everyone around you.

The spirit of gossip has jumped on so many people without them even knowing it. Gossip interferes with love. It gets in the way of love. It interrupts our divine connection to receiving more love. Those who gossip all the time usually also lack patience and self love. When you love yourself, you do not need to talk about anyone in order to make yourself feel good. If they are that bad just get away from them. Don't allow yourself to be in situations that hinder your own personal growth. Start thinking about you and your partner.

Take the time to do something nice for your partner or even someone else with no expectations. When you have no expectations from the love you release, love continues to flow unto you freely. When love knows that you are loving just because that is what you want and desire; it completely changes the game up. Completely.

GUYS THE LADIES LOVE YOU, BUT YOU HAVE A FEW THINGS THAT NEED SOME

ATTENTION

Goddess Moni

Chapter 6
STOP BEING A MODERN DAY JODY!

In other words, if you are a Jody you are male version of a side chick. You refuse to be responsible or accountable for having your own anything, so you settle for the role of baby boy while your weekly routine consists of you being a Jody! You have no respect for women nor men, when she turns you down, and lets you know that she has a man instead of you respecting that you proceed with, "*I am sure that your man does not mind if you have a friend or not.*' Responses like this is exactly why women have gone the route of ignoring this type of stupidity.

You are so bad at hitting on her that when she ignores you out of respect of her man, you call her a stuck up bitch. You are choosing to not care about how disrespectful that you are being towards women. This is not the way for you to have a woman as long as you are on this path of being disrespectful, the only thing that it will do is turn her off. No real woman wants nor desires to have any man that behaves as a Jody, especially when she knows of her own value and worth.

The thing about Jody that has him drawing women even if it is temporary is the fact that Jody does all that she wants her permanent man to do.

Jody is a modern day male side dude.

1. Jody wants to spend time with her.
2. Jody listens to all of her problems silently.
3. Jody invites her kids over to show her that all of her matters to him.
4. Jody is willing to be a man even if he has not figured out what that is yet.
5. Jody values what her permanent man overlooks

Jody has a problem though:

1. Jody wants another man's woman.
2. Jody hates being responsible, he just appears to be on the surface.

3. Jody wants to have fun, he is not thinking longevity.
4. Jody has not reached the pinnacle of his own manhood yet.
5. Jody is not thinking about the hearts of anyone involved in the situation
6. Jody does not want the permanent position of her man

Jody is a modern day male side dude. Jody knows this, but he does not care. He is willing to be a side dude, because he can send her home to her permanent man. He wants to help her keep her permanent man so he does not have to deal with being accountable for the permanent man's position.

    I hate to burst your bubble ladies, but some of you are with Jody and you do not even have a permanent man. Stop expecting a permanent position from a temporary man. Jody is not built for permanent, he is built for temporary. Accept this or you will waste your own time. Now if you only want a man to get you through a tough season then Jody is your guy. He will get you through it, in fact he has been waiting for your man to screw up just to get you through it. Jody is a broke version of a Sugar Daddy without the sugar and he understands getting his way all you way. His objective is him.

On the outside Jody appears to be confident, but Jody has a desire to be loved, and he has been looking for it in all the wrong places. Jody does not trust in his own ability to attract a real woman in his life anymore. Of course Jody would love to have a permanent woman, but you have to know that trust left Jody long before he became your side dude. A guy name Jody knows that the thirst is all too real.

My personal experience, I don't like Jody's. These type of men have no respect for relationships. Their idea of hitting on you is saying, *"Does your man mind you having a friend?"* He is pushy and lacks all forms of any class. He pretends to have it going on, but deep down inside he knows he has nothing to keep you. Every woman has experienced a Jody even if it means that she just blew him off. She knows that he responds to her with such an attitude as if you are supposed to give him your number just because he desires to have it. Jody can be very confusing as he gives off the air of confidence, but it is only what he gives off. Jody just does not like to experience or feel being rejected.

WHO IS JODY'S COMPETITOR?

Jody's competitor is the permanent man. The permanent man is the one who brings the bacon (turkey not pork) home for his woman to fry it. The permanent man is confident. He trusts. and knows that his woman is not going anywhere. He is a real man. He is strong in will power. He works hard for what he wants and he strives for perfection on a daily basis. He is not afraid of his own mistakes, yet he does not want to repeat them either.

Permanent men know that Jody's exist, yet they feel that if Jody can have her then he might as well keep her. The same goes with a real woman, she knows if a side chick can have him then she might as well keep him.

Individuals with permanent positions are not interested in having a side chick or a side dude, they understand the energy that it takes from building their empire. Every time you enter into a relationship whether temporary or long term it will still require a certain level of your energy. Be wise about this, you don't want to wake up one day tired of giving yourself away when you could have poured your energy into one relationship and received a huge harvest in return. You have to watch where you are sewing your seed, make sure that the faith of your love falls on fertile ground.

Jody has tricks and distractions to draw you towards him. It is all a ploy to keep you there on a temporary basis. He is not thinking of the emotions that can be involved with having a real relationship. He has not even thought about going this far with you. Jody knows in his mind that he is still a boy himself that just wants to play, temporary house with you. If you want to be happy, tell Jody deuces.

Chapter 7
POWER IN EMPIRE

The hit reality show titled, 'Empire' has become one of the top must see shows in the year of 2014. I jumped in on watching the 2015 season. Individuals all over the world stopped what they were doing to turn to the Fox Network to watch Cookie and Lucious Lion. They are prime example of the human desire in today's society to have and to build an empire.

Although the two characters on the show are no longer together it has become a goal for relationships to not only build strong foundations, but to become power couples, powerhouses, with the main objective being for them to build an Empire. Minus the bullshit.

    All individuals who have a vision desire to be with someone not only in whom they can share it with, but someone that they know that they can trust their vision with. As a woman on a consistent path of building a legacy, empire, and pushing harder to get things done it has always been my desire to build it with someone on the same page as one and in unison. When you are able to sit and plan things together it completely changes your outlook, how you do things, and why you are doing what you do. If you are in a relationship and that person is not inspiring you to go harder or getting you to look at the person that stares you in the face daily (self) then you are obviously missing out on something. You should be provoking one another to reach your goals daily, weekly, and monthly.

There is power in the number (2), yes you are strong alone, however when you add +1 you become even stronger. There is strength in numbers. Work towards having team effort, then the two of you will accomplish what you are working on entirely faster. This is not to say that you need to rush, this is to say that you need to be (SMART) about your work.

"Two are better than (1), for if one falls the other will be there to pick the (1) up"

At some point in your life, you will begin to strive towards building a powerhouse with your partner as a couple. There will only be a few that understand the power of moving in this direction. It is so important that when you strive on this path as a couple to make sure that what you have personally is solid. If your personal relationship is not yet strong enough then building a business together is a very bad idea. It is hard to maintain any business between two partners that do not even know how to get along.

Power couples business is based upon you being a power couple, therefore the two of you have to be on the same wave length of spiritual communication that way no matter what you are you able to speak, feel, and vibe from the vibrations of one another. Their energy connects. As a power couple the two of you must focus on being so strategic about praying and meditating. These practices will increase the two of you ability to be in sync with one another.

Power couples behave completely differently than average couples as they:

1. They have weekly meetings with one another.
2. They set goals and milestones to reach.
3. They focus on building.

4. They flirt legally during boss up meetings without the risk of sexual harassment lawsuits. Laughing!
5. They are happier because they are blessed with the opportunity to build with the one in whom they love dearly.
6. They admire the drive and ambition of one another.
7. They stay up late dreaming, planning, and acting towards their vision.
8. They are still working their vision when the rest of the world has stopped, went to sleep, or doing what everyone else is doing.
9. They are opportunist with one another and with those that they meet.
10. They are hard workers. They enjoy the abundance of vacations together while appreciating every minute that they are sharing together.
11. They are consumed with vision.

Building an empire will not be easy, however if you do have a partner that exudes the same power that you have then go ahead and enforce being a #power-couple now.

More Power will always exist in duality. Get on the same page and ride the wave of your power, your success, and keep the momentum going as you love the life that you are living.

Chapter 8
WITHOUT TRUST YOU HAVE NOTHING

You cannot love anyone until you accept the fact that love does not exist without trust. God has given us all this love and when we operate in purpose the only way for this love to function properly is for you to trust in it. It means nothing to the spirit of God when we do not trust the spirit within you with your life, your decisions, and your heart. We do not function properly when we refuse to give in to this love that is cherished with an abundance of trust. When we learn to trust God this is the only time that a relationship will work out. In our ability to trust God we also open ourselves to loving and trusting your partner.

I was horrible at trusting anyone. I had been hurt so many times in my life that it felt like a never ending cycle that was on spin. It is not just relationships with a man or woman that hurt us, it could come from a friend, a parent, a cousin, or anyone close to you. Hurt is often buried deep inside of us and it is often hard to find out later on in life that we are still holding on to the same things.

Anger + Pain is all just a spirit that seeks to destroy the love inside of individuals. Anger knows that every time that you agree with it you are releasing some of your blessings out of your life. The first time that someone told moi that every time I allowed myself to reach anger that I would also be giving away my blessings, it became hard really fast for someone to make moi upset with them. I wish I knew this back when. Ok! Hello!

During the learning process:

It seemed like no matter what I did, the wheels just kept spinning round and round. My fear to let someone in and trust them with my heart was literally eating moi alive. There was no one to blame anyone, but myself. It does not matter how many times you have been hurt, you cannot carry all that pain and junk with you. All pain does is continue to build up in your heart just for it to one day release itself into the lives of someone innocent who has never done anything to hurt you. It is sad that this happens, but the truth is that many of us are unaware that we are still holding on to pain.

If you want to be successful at life, love, and relationships then you will need to surround yourself with individuals who do not mind speaking life into your greatness without sugar coating anything. As adults sometimes we forget to allow individuals that don't mind getting in our space to allow us to change for the greater good. I am not saying that when someone loves you that they should just spit out a bunch of negativity. I am saying that if they see something that is holding you back they should tell you. There is no real reason for you to get mad at them about it. If they did not love you, they would not tell you at all. These individuals are the ones who set you free to receive your promises. As the saying goes, "*The truth hurts,*" *but why live blind when you have the power and ability to see?*

The truth is an open door to our healing and our future. My trust issues were embedded deep, way into my childhood where the thoughts of my father being the first man to ever walk out of my life was just sitting in my heart. I just wanted someone to love moi. This statement was my very downfall, it caused moi to rush and to lose. It caused moi to be someone that I wasn't, for many years I was conforming to what others wanted from moi out of fear of losing them when they could have cared less of losing moi. Don't be afraid to love! Love yourself first! As I grew into a mature love I grew into loving without expecting anything in return.

The best love relationship is when the two partners only fear is the fear of losing one another because they will work to keep one another through love, self-love, compromise, duality, oneness, support, loyalty, and faithfulness.

KEY INGREDIENT: LOVE YOURSELF MORE AND YOUR RELATIONSHIP WILL REMAIN HEALTHY!

I knew that I had given my energy into the wrong relationships. In return I had to deal with the bad decisions that I made. I had to learn that true success does not come in anything including a relationship when there is a lack of wisdom. Life allows us all to experience pain, failure, and other things to teach us to value the success, the wealth, the love, the fame, and whatever else that you are blessed with.

God will take away anyone or anything that you love more than than the spirit in you. God's spirit is within us all, when you love who you are that is when you can love your partner with a great love that God intended for you to share. You pay a price for love and the ticket is steep if you are serious about going for it. Love will cost you time, energy, devotion, dedication, trust, loyalty, respect, and effort. Before you set yourself on a path to love anyone you must ask yourself, *"Are you willing to pay the cost?"*

It is time that you make a decision to set yourself free from your own bondage, pain, and insecurities. It is time to let go and fly. For moi it was just time that I started taking giant leaps in faith with nothing holding moi back. It was time that I did something for myself that would benefit my family greatly. I had to show myself some damn love and stop worrying about a man. If it is meant for you to have a man or woman in your life that is what God will bless you with.

Exude the character of a person of great patience.

Your journey will take you some time, but be patent with yourself. No one can love you until you love you. Somewhere along the way between myself, the hell, and heart ache I stopped loving moi the way that I started out. Bad situations, bad choices, bad decisions, and failed relationships (family & friends) had destroyed my confidence and my ability to trust anyone. I knew that I wanted to have a real relationship with my father.

I had to focus on regaining this love for myself. I began trusting the spirit of God to step in and give moi the desires of my own heart.

After all at the end of the day the only thing that you can do is step out on faith, once you step out God gives you the increase. Stop being afraid like I was and start stepping towards a rewarding future. Regain your strength and your confidence! All of these years have went by and evil has been stealing your joy over and over again. Evil has been raping you from your future. We have all been assaulted blindly. It is time to wake up to let evil know that enough is enough.

At that point of saying enough is enough, you have to get up, and do something that will make you feel good on the inside. You are a survivor. You have survived hell and now it is time that you accept the fact that you are gorgeous, beautiful, smart, intelligent, handsome, and far more important; You are powerful. Trust in this with everything in you.

One of the greatest thing that someone close to moi has ever done for moi was tell moi that if I could not trust, I could not love. The two go hand and hand. They told moi I would be the only one who could get to the root of why I was not loving. I had to do some personal digging. I decided to take 30 Days just to dig inside of myself.

God began to yield unto moi the fruit of the womb: **Trust**

Day 1 Be slow to speak and quick to hear

Day 2 There is nothing wrong with letting go of your ideas or ways of doing things

Day 3 You can't be in love and be in control at the same time

Day 4 Love only works with trust. Be fair about it.

Day 5 God will give you someone that you never had, don't judge it by looking through the lens of your past.

Day 6 Patience is the key to unlock the doors of your own blessing

Day 7 Every problem has a solution, but first you must find the problem or you will just be fixing nothing.

Day 8 You still don't get it

Day 9 Love is right there

Day 10 Whatever may be missing can be found in you.

Day 11 Open your eyes

Day 12 Just be thankful

Day 13 God does everything for a reason

Day 14 It is only a test. God will work it out

Day 15 Knowing what you trust is everything

Day 16 Trusting God with your life is essential not just in word but in deed and in action

Day 17 It seems worse than what it really is

Day 18 Prayer is everything in the season that you are in, it is training you for your future

Day 19 It is not all about you

Day 20 Handle your Business, Stop looking at your partner

Day 21 Spend some time in prayer and mediation

Day 22 Know what you are supposed to be doing

Day 23 Stay Focused

Day 24 Keep it Simple Shawty

Day 25 Less is More

Day 26 Its not that serious

Day 27 God has your Back

Day 28 Trust in God's will for your life, not anyone else's. Be accountable for your purpose alone

Day 29 Embrace your Power

Day 30 In God's timing all things are perfected

What I was learning most was that time flies and you better get the most out of it, because everyday God is blessing you. Pay attention. In order to appreciate who God gives you must first appreciate the love that God has already given you. God is adding unto you each & everyday that is how much the spirit of God loves you. All you have to do is appreciate what he gives you everyday with praise and a simple Thank You. When you are able to rejoice in the time of adversity then God moves even more to bless you. Rejoice when you are tired. Rejoice when it makes no sense. Rejoice without cause or reason- rejoice!

Sometimes the only thing that you are missing is a *"Thank You."* This could change your life, your relationship, and your success. Appreciate and value all the small things, because you will only be attacked by the same very small things. It is the small things that get you to the big places. It is the small things that get your greatest love to love you even more. The small things are the very things that continue to add up. All success is made through small steps not giant ones.

 A very valuable lesson that I learned in my own personal journey is that it is not always how you feel, sometimes what you feel has absolutely nothing to do with your partner. How you feel belongs to you and not them. You must learn to be accountable for your own feelings, stop blaming your partner for things that you are thinking. What you are thinking could be the furthest thing from their mind. Too often we confuse feelings with intuition, because we all were taught that our intuition is like a feeling that we get at the bottom of our stomach. And sometimes this is very true, but there are other feelings that are attached to our emotions alone that are triggered when we see something that may be a mini spectacle of our past. This type of feeling and thought will destroy your relationship.

Change your thought patterns and stop accusing your thoughts on your partner.

#MoniAdvice

Not everyone who is out late at night is screwing.

Not everyone who is out of town on business is cheating.

Not everyone that compliments you wants you.

Not every man who gets upset is an abuser.

Not everyone woman with kids is a hoe.

Not every man struggling is a loser.

Not every man with a penis is a cheater.

Not every woman with a vagina wants to control you with it.

Not every man with money is a trick.

Not every woman with financial goals is a gold digger.

Not every older woman and man has wisdom. IJS!

Stop assuming things that someone taught you. Half of what someone has told you has been based on a theory. Stop taking advice from old miserable, ass bitches who are teaching girls that being a woman is having a bad attitude and being half naked. Stop listening to old ass, trick men who are telling you to get multiple women when they are paying for pussy. The quicker you understand this the better. Listen to women who understand their value. Listen to men who value women.

If you don't give your partner the opportunity to love you then you may just miss out on their love. It is up to you, nevertheless give trust a shot; trust gave it to you, give it back. It is only fair.

Chapter 9
SHUT UP & DRIVE

Everyone wants to be heard, but the two of you need to shut the hell up, and allow the person that is driving to do just that. There is a lot to be said about two powerful individuals who love one another yet they are clueless as to how to shut up and just get in the presence of one another's beauty and allow their love and soul to just glow. No no wins when the two of you want to win individually, both of you need to give in to the greater good of the relationship. God has joined the two of you together to show forth his love and kindness. Why are the two of you being mean to one another? Why are the two of you destroying a bond that is so strong just because you have your own way of doing things? We all can sit and harp on things day after day, but the truth is that it is not getting you anywhere. Ask yourself, *"Why are you doing this to yourself, your partner, and your relationship?*

The two of you have been chosen for one another. The two of you are far more stronger together than you are apart. Who cares if both of you know how to be independent, you and your mate are suffering and it is all centered around your inability to let go + a desire to just prove a point. *"Is it even worth it to prove a point?"* Once that point is proven, the two of you would have created an entirely new damage to your relationship that will only make it harder for the both of you to reap the harvest and the reward that is in place for the two of you only. You have to evaluate your own thoughts, ways of thinking before you just project those feelings on your partner. Great decision makers calculate the cost along with the risk, which means that they realize that they are thinkers that need to analyze their own thoughts first. Excellent decision makers know how to move in faith.

If you are still living off of the fact that there are more fish in the sea, more women, or more men then you still have not matured as an adult yet. There should be no other than your partner, your soul mate, there is no one like him or her. Why are you tearing down your own empire with words that are killing what the two of you have planted?

Stop being childish and start functioning as the adults that you are. You can act as a spoiled brat everyday if you want, but kicking and screaming has never gotten a grown ass adult anywhere. The two of you are on an emotional roller coaster and you are losing, because both of you want to get your point across. The two of you need to snap out of it before the best opportunities, the best relationship, and the best love of your life is no longer in your life. Someone has to take a stand, why not take a stand together?

The two of you are as close to perfection as the two of you are going to get, so stop complaining about something that is so petty. It is not even worth losing one another over. It is very important for the two of you to understand that only one person can drive at a time. The best way for the two of you to reach this place is to recognize your individual strengths and weakness and to allow one another to operate in what you are strong at. The areas that you are weak in, allow your partner the space to flow in. Don't fight against what you know is your partners strength. This will become the beauty in your relationship. Working together is a whole lot easier than a desire to be in control of your love life. Let that shit go. Love your partner. Trust their strength, know your own weakness.

Chapter 10

IF IT AIN'T ABOUT THE MONEY, DON'T BE BLOWING ME UP! DON'T BE WASTING MY TIME!

-TI

Money is the number one reason couples break up according to Statistic Brain. If money is the number one reasons for breakups then, *"Why in the hell are the two of you splitting up about something that is so petty? Why are you destroying something over something so minor?* The two of you can get past anything as long as the two of you are willing to get past anything.

9 times out 10 if you are not arguing about money the two of you are probably money making power houses and something small is working to split the two of you apart to keep the success of what you are building from flowing. The question is, *"Are the two of you going to focus on getting to this money or what?"* If you are arguing about something that is not adding up, then you are just wasting time arguing about nothing. Deal with it, let it go, and keep it moving. Time is something that once you waste it, you will not earn it back.

If the two of you cannot get on the same page it does not matter how much of a powerhouse the two of you are. When couples are not able to agree they will not be able to earn money together.

We must stop living life so irresponsibly like we are children. If you want and desire to win then you must start acting like winners in your relationships. Winners don't quit when it hurts, they keep going. It is a plus when you are able to keep going when it hurts, this is what makes you strong. When you give up when it hurts, you automatically tear down what you have been working towards and working on. I gave up on relationships due to the fact that I just did not want to push past the pain. If that is what you want to do, then do it however don't let go of a great relationship just based off the fact that you don't want to work at it anymore. Ask yourself is the prize that you will gain bigger than what you are fighting over? If the prize is bigger, then keep going.

If the prize is smaller, then by all means stop working at it. There is nothing else for you to discuss.

As I am writing this book, I noticed that there were two couples sitting right next to moi in Starbucks. A couple in front of moi who announced that they were also business partners. A couple on the right of moi who announced that they were marketers creating a strategy for a client. This was an eye opener of the realm of possibilities of what two can do when they come together as a power house. As I continued to watch, I picked up one great thing that they were willing to sit until they were done doing the work that had to be completed. They had a bond that was noticeable. They knew one another's strengths and they knew one another's weaknesses.

Many times in relationships we complain about our partners strengths and weaknesses, when we can create a way to make them work.

Observation of Couple #1:

As I continued to observe I noticed that the woman opened the meetings with a pleasant greet and an offer to buy the potential client coffee. Once she completed the introduction, her partner took over. They knew one another first before the individual in whom they had to meet with even came into the picture.

Observation of Couple #2:

Now the other couple, could not come to an agreement, then they decided to quit. The male handed his partner back her notebook and said, "*I am done with it.*" She replied, "*Well I am not changing my mind and I am going to go ahead and email them.*" The two got up and walked away.

They did not understand how to come to a mutual agreement with one another, they gave up, they quit, because they lacked the ability to exercise in patience plus an understanding of one another's strengths and weakness. This is horrible! Individuals' need to learn that if it is worth having, it is worth the strategy, the technique, and the wait. This is the way the two of you are going to make more money x more money = more money.

> *Individuals need to learn that if it is worth having, it is worth the strategy, the technique, and the wait.*

Don't miss out on your money! Don't start a great race with a great partner and lose out on what God is doing for the both of you. When you conquer your own spirituality in the spiritual realm you are soon to conquer the financial realm. The two of you deserve to embrace the beauty of your greatness. You need to know that there is power in the love that the two of you share. No one likes to lose, yet individuals make decisions to do so every single day. It makes absolutely no sense, none what so ever.

Stop destroying what the two of you have built. The two of you are incredible, but the two of you need to recognize that the love you have has been given to you by God and not the spirit of lust. Some men and women have spent so much time in their life lusting that they have no clue as to how to accept real love when it comes to them. They fight the best thing in their life from comparing it to the worse things that have ever happened to them. We all are guilty of this pleasure. We all have fallen short at some point and time in our life.

It is time to stop falling down over and over again and time to just live your life as royalty. You are awesome and if you want what is powerful and great just make a decision to keep going! Money over BS! If it ain't about the money, then don't be blowing moi up! Stop blowing your partner up over something that is so simple. Acknowledge the problem, solve it, and then agree to change it. Don't waste time holding on to religion, arguing your own perspectives, and ideas that are only pushing your partner further and further away from you. Get to that paper!

Chapter 11

IT TAKES TWO TO MAKE A THING GO RIGHT. IT TAKES TWO TO MAKE IT OUT OF SIGHT.

You ever notice the major difference between old school music and today's music? Today's music is missing the key ingredient of love. We all would like to think that love does not matter anymore or that it is irrelevant, but it is important to remember that it takes love to make love. It takes two to tango and if only one is pouring out love then something is wrong with that picture. We don't often get to experience the luxury of our relationships being perfect and they are not suppose to be. We are not perfect human beings. We all have flaws and issues along with things that we still want to figure out. Just know that being in love with someone is not played out and that chivalry is not dead. Living a life of balance is very important to your relationship. It is also important if you are not in a relationship. Balance is your female + male side flowing within your body to give you an understanding of yourself and of your partner.

 Women and men both make the sacrifice for the chance at love. Women leave everything that they know for men everyday and this is something that should be valued. Men do this as well just not as often as women do, so when a man has a woman that is going the extra distance to be with him, he needs to pay attention before he loses her. This is working together as two. Same thing with the woman, if he is going the distance for you she needs to pay attention before she loses him. We take so much for granted. We get so comfortable with ourselves and our partners that we forget to go that extra mile for one another.

 Don't ever feel like holding back in a relationship, because if that is how you feel all that you are doing is holding your partner up. Think about your partner in your decision making. Sometimes we forget due to the fear of being alone, however you are not alone anymore. There is someone else is in your life. It is almost like having a new baby and not being considerate that they are there. A new relationship requires change, time, and adjustment. If you are not willing to make these changes then you are not willing to make the sacrifice to make the relationship work.

It is not about losing yourself to this person, it is about the fact that you are sharing your time and space with someone else and knowing that this is a very sensitive space for the two of you not just one of you. Although we want to verbalize how we feel to our partner, sometimes they are not ready to listen to what you have to say to them. We must stay prepared to exercise patience in order to understand that you are dealing with two identities, two perspectives, and sometimes two different lifestyles.

> No prior situation can prepare you for a new human being.

No prior situation can prepare you for a new being. This is so important, because so many of us start over thinking that we have been through enough to understand and to get this person, but this is only a false way of thinking. Your partner has different DNA, a different past, different experiences, different beliefs, and to go in thinking that you know this person so well based off of your past experiences you are only setting the relationship up for failure. This is the worse thing that you can do, take the time to get to know your partner. Take the time to learn of them. Do not compare them to your past failures, those were your mistakes, not the person that you are with. This is very important. We go in relationships blaming, suggesting, and guessing that we know all that there is to know about this one being that we miss out on what makes them so unique and special. You cannot think that judging them with a blind perspective will help your relationship. This is not the way to live, eventually you will not only drive yourself crazy but you will drive your partner out of your life.

We do it all the time, everyday in fact, and we think that it is cool even though it is not at all.

> *"Is knowing what you have enough or do you need to be reminded of what you have on the regular?"*

When two individuals establish the value of their connection, their purpose then they also will establish the importance of reminding one another of how much having their love in their life means. Love is all God. We must never forget that. We have to securely establish our connection with God in order to trust our connection with mankind. In order to do this, we must forget what we think and get in tune with our God connection and increase the focus on what is in you. Anytime you meet a person that makes you feel the need to increase your connection with God in order for you to relate to them, they are your soul mate.

Again I began to see the blessing through listening to what someone else had to say to moi that hit home. I learned from pure guidance. I was being shown the distance that I needed to go for God. It was teaching to moi trust in God's will. I had work to do and I knew that this would only be the beginning of my journey. My goal for 30 Days was to work on increasing my ability to trust God with my life, not just part of it, but my entire life.

Regardless of who you are, you cannot trust in the will of the one that you are with without trusting the will that God has giving them. Trust is the lifeline of your love relationship.

All love and hate relationships lack trust that is why the other part to that love is hate. This is only a doubled edge sword that will eventually stab the both of you, because eventually the hate will turn on one of you without thinking twice of why it even moved forward in the act itself. Make a decision. Either you love or hate the one that you are with, you cannot do both.

Chapter 12
MAKE SURE THAT GOD IS THE 3RD CORD IN YOUR RELATIONSHIP

It does not matter who you are, where you are from, it is vital that you make sure that God is the 3 cord of your relationship or it will not work. God is the head of all that you will ever do, regardless of your background, your history, your culture, likes, dislikes, or your current situation. God is the spirit that is within each one of us and when we decide that we are ready to have a partner, we also need to make a decision that God has to remain the 3rd cord that connects us as one. God is the glue that bonds the two of you together. He is the protection that will hold the two of you together when you face any storm in your life.

I use to wonder all the time, *"How do my grandparents stick together the way that they do and they continue to do year after year?"* I could not for the life of moi after failed relationships, heart ache, and all the lack of understanding I had experienced figure out what was it that I just did not get about holding it together. Then it came to moi only when I was ready to hear the truth of what was holding moi back. I was not allowing the spirit of God to be the other cord in my life. God will carry you through situations and storms that were designed to literally rip your life into shreds and leave you for death.

God is the very thing that makes the difference in you being alive and you being left stranded in the middle of no where with no clue in the world as to what is going on. And I hate to be the barrier of this news, but the way for it to work is for you to have that 3rd spiritual cord. We have all tried our own way without the spirit and have seen the mass destruction that it has caused and created in our life. The question is, *"Are you tired of the mistakes, living below your means, living an average life, knowing that the spirit of God has called you to a greater life?"*

It is hard to say that we all have been chosen to live a great life it is like saying everyone is chosen to be drafted into the NFL. Everyone is not chosen, there has to be something that you show whether in your skills, your ability to train hard, your willingness to listen, or your ability to stay motivated when everyone else wants to throw in the towel. It is even more important to remember that working hard at being great does not stop unless you no longer desire it.

Everyone does not have the same stamina and will power to go when others want to stop going. Individuals have to have the will power to live a chosen life. This is what God has called you out your past into where you are were born to be.

God is the same way in your life and in your relationship, and if you keep putting the spirit of God down then what holds the two of you together becomes weak and what was once together could easily fall completely apart. You do not want this to ever happen, therefore let God remain the pilot. Stop

Your relationship belongs to the love not to either one of you.

wanting to be the one in control. Your relationship belongs to the love not to either one of you. If the two of you can remember this it will hold you both to a bond that is unable to be broken. It will allow the two of you to enjoy the love.

As human beings we make being in the arms of God one of the most difficult things that we could ever do, but once it is done it is one of the most simplest decisions that we could ever make. You are now challenged to let go and to let the love that the two of you have lead the relationships. This means throwing away pointless thoughts, what you are use to, and any and all negativity that you could think of or come up with. All these things do is bring destruction to you. When you treat your relationship like you do your professional life you will be in for a real treat. Again what it all boils down to is, *"How much success do you really want to flow in your lives together?"*

Chapter 13

THE HEART

The Distance between my heart and my mind.

ALL WOMEN HAVE A MASCULINE SIDE! ALL MEN HAVE A FEMINE SIDE!

As I cut my grass today, I could feel every ounce of religion, tradition, and my old ways of doing things being broken in moi. There is nothing like the thought when something breaks that has had you in bondage for years.

The more I continued to do things that I felt like a man should be doing for moi, the more. I could feel the emotions of being lost, somewhere unfamiliar, and I felt myself moving into an entirely new territory as I felt everything including the individuals in whom could not understand what I was going through. There was a reason for all that I was feeling.

Things I never saw myself doing:

1. Cutting grass

2. Looking under the hood of my car

3. Putting air in my tire

4. Fixing things

     I could remember conversing with one of my mentors as he told moi that every woman has a masculine side, when she does something that a man usually does it helps her to be able to understand him. The same goes for men when they do something that is feminine (such as cooking, helping out with housework, etc), it helps them understand her.

None of us are able to know the depths of how one individual can feel unless we have personally been there. God was allowing moi to feel things that I had never felt before. The more I became thankful openly, I felt like the more pain I felt inwardly, the spirit was healing my life from everything. When you are being healed you will all feel the pain from what you are being healed from.

I was learning that the spirit had no idea of male, female, religion, skin color, or our ideas of how to do things. As a mature woman I felt like my life was different from the way that it was designed to be on many days. I wanted to not complain, nor cry, nor feel hurt as I began to understand life.

God wanted moi to understand the male mind by doing the things that a man would do. I was beginning to see that as women sometimes we take for granted what men do for us. I saw that there were some things that I took for granted in my life that I could not recognize, because I was taught that how I was doing it was the way that it was suppose to be done. My ideas were being broken into million of pieces, before God could bless moi with my eternity. I had to know the depths of how to love, respect, and honor without taking anything for granted.

God was changing my heart, it was being healed, and released into a higher capacity that would help moi to be able to handle anything that would come my way. God had given moi a heart to love a counter part on the level that the spirit of God would love on. All this time I would think that it was other things that were in my way, however I was in my own way. It was my own heart that was not open to receive, because I had allowed it to get cold along the way. My heart was going through a complete transformation that I knew nothing about.

LEARN TO KNOW YOUR HEART!

There are certain things that men and woman desire when they are in a relationship and when either one of them feel as though their needs are not being met then they tend to consider other options. It is the truth, no one desires to be in a relationship and still feel like they are alone. If you are in a long distance relationship and your partner is showing no type of connection nor missing you then you might want to leave your options open. IJS when you reach a certain age and a person who loves you begins to not show that he or she loves you there is something wrong.

A man and a woman who cares for you will show you even if it is in his own way. There are some men out there who are quiet, there are some men who verbalize their feelings, and there are those men who show how they feel through physical touch and affection when they see you. Don't judge him Don't judge her! Get to know the person that you desire. It is so easy for men and women to put up a front to try to impress the person in whom they desire, but it is even harder to keep up and maintain. This is why it is important to allow your partner to be comfortable with you. If your partner fears losing you and you are their heart's desire it can end up being a compromising situation. Individuals often desire to please the person in whom they desire. Regardless of how they respond to what you have to say if they make you feel a certain way, your feelings must matter enough to you if not at all to him or her. The heart just work like this once the feelings are involved. If your partner ignores your feelings then maybe you need to think whether or not you really want the relationship or not, if you do then the two of you need to have a one on one about how either you are feeling or how the two of you are feeling. If the relationship lacks the ability to relate and connect then it lacks the ability for the two hearts to become one. Men and women both play games, although I know that men are not so well at playing those games as they think that they are, and when they do think they are playing well -Ladies hit them out of the blue. Men never feel like you are getting away with anything. She knows and she is now playing to win. At this point in the game of hearts for her winning is making his ass feel worse than he made her feel. Why? That is just what the heart does when you make it feel a certain way sometimes. When you are playing the game as a player make sure that you know that one day you will meet your dare devil match. If at all possible chose to love over playing games. When you play games eventually you will receive a dose of your own medicine.

Life is un-fair sometimes, but only because that is how we make it. We make bad decisions that we have to live with. The great thing about it is that we can stop right where we are and make better decisions. Choices can change. You can go on a better path starting immediately. Why not start now?

He either loves or he doesn't?

He either loves you or he doesn't?

She either loves or she doesn't?

She either loves you or she doesn't?

That is just the way the cookie crumbles.

Just to go a little deeper of asking yourself, *"Can you change these thoughts that try to disturb you? Are they just thoughts of negativity that are trying to come through you?"* Most days our mind is extremely active, this is something that I had to battle with on so many levels. I was working to fight against these voices that were in my head that caused moi to feel certain things and I had to learn what provoked certain thoughts. No one wants to go through life with any negative thought in their head period so learning how to allow those thoughts to just pass through my body was extremely important. Self control.

      All that we do is on a dimensional level. We are constantly going through different dimensions in our life even if we dislike what we are going through the best thing for is to do is to quickly allow it to pass through our bodies. It is not for us to fight every thought that comes to us. Some thoughts are just spirits that are seeking a body that will believe in it. We take on these negative spirits, negative entities, and we begin to fight a raging war with something that has come with the purpose just to frustrate us. We take on the characteristic of these entities without even realizing what we are doing so, even though they are coming out of the blue. Things come to us to distract us and to test our ability to keep going regardless of what the thing itself is.

If you truly want success in and at anything you must first learn to overcome the emotions that are in your head and not your heart. The emotions that are in your head are totally opposite than the ones that are in your heart. Don't be deceived by deceiving entities.

If all else fails in life there are two options for you to either sit still or to keep going. If you learn to do both at the same time well that makes you a brilliant warrior. I set myself on a path to do both. Moving forward is everything, but learning to sit still when it is taking place will release all things unto you.

If we can grasp this science we are half way through from where we are to where we desire to be. Whatever your heart desires will be yours within arms reach. Quoted by Juanita Bynum, *"Whatever has been willed in your heart, everything that is within 10 feet of your heart has to come under subjection to the will that is in your heart."*

This is why your purpose has to manifest itself in those around you in whom are apart of that very will must come to acknowledge the power that is within you. The power that is within you will help you to obtain success in your relationship as well as in your life, if someone in your life is against the will that is in your heart then their time in your life becomes limited.

The power that is within you will help you to obtain success in your relationship as well as in your life, if someone in your life is against the will that is in your heart then their time in your life becomes limited.

your life becomes limited. Even if it hurts you to lose them, all things that have been set with a purpose in you has to come forward. All things. Stay focused on the prize. You are winning!

Chapter 14
STOP BEING SELFISH

Somewhere along the way someone told us that by us being selfish that we win. In the mix of us trying or attempting to grasp this understanding we confuse being selfish with loving ourselves and protecting our purpose. I knew that I had been selfish many days of my life and the spoil brat in moi did not care about how it affected others. I wanted what I wanted, if I did not get what I wanted it put moi in a bad mood. This is when selfishness was at work in moi before I matured as a woman and as a leader. I am a charitable individual. I uplift as many individuals as possible to live the greatest life ever. This is not what I am referring to. I am referring to the fact that when we are in relationships we think more about how we can please ourselves than how we can please our partner. We want the glory out of the things that we are doing. This all made moi truly think about love in general. God has been quoted to want the glory from our lives, for us to live, and to glorify the spirit through it all and at the end of it all we will all in fact receive this glory.

 When I began to truly evaluate the two it made more sense of what the spirit within us does for us to receive glory than what we do on the physical realm to receive glory. The spirit of God does not think of itself, in fact it releases blessing within us to show us the power of its love for us. The spirit of God does not want nor desire anything from us that we are not desiring to give up freely.

The spirit of God desires our love, but not through the spirit of selfishness. When you are selfish, in return you receive nothing. Love is the gift that offers more gifts unto your freely.

In relationships we have to learn to be a blessing to our partners through the love that we have for them to not receive anything, but to do so just out of our love for them. This is why God {Universe} is able to receive glory out of our life. Certain individuals wake up and they love God anyway, regardless of their situation, regardless of what they are going through, they love the spirit that they dwell in, and they know that staying in the presence of the spirit itself is the greatest feeling in the world.

When you reach a level of maturity that has no time cap on it, you begin to do things just to be a blessing. You are not looking at whether or not the other person may or may not reciprocate the same feelings towards you, however your love is your blessing, and when you release it, the universe has to release it back to you. Sometimes your blessings are withheld due to the fact that you are more focused on what you want to receive verses what you can do to be a blessing. The movie Fireproof was a huge advocate of this very lesson, as the man in the movie started thinking more about his wife in return he could enjoy their love. For as long as selfishness was present it held the two of them back from receiving the power of love.

The purpose of any and all relationships is to show forth truth and love, don't forget this. If your relationship is not showing forth truth and love then it is still missing the spirit of God as an ingredient.

Ask yourself today:

1. How can I show my partner that I am not thinking about myself?

2. Are you showing the spirit that is within you the same energy?

3. When is the last time you told your partner that you were proud of them?

4. Do you have thoughts of jealousy when you partner achieves their goals or are you jealous of their accomplishments?

5. Do you focus more on what your partner can do for you or on what you can do for your partner?

You don't win being selfish, you win through being charitable with your love, and with a partner who is already pre-existing a spirit to reciprocate the same love. I want to make this clear, so individuals don't just give away their love to the wrong individual and get upset when it destroys them. We have all done so this is why it is important for us to stop at some point and release this only to the one who has been purposed to be on the receiving end. This is the one that gave up their free will to share their life, their love, and their space with you. This is the one that will help you to know, *"Love is something you do for someone else, not something you do for yourself."*

Chapter 15

IS GOOGLE THE NEW RELATIONSHIP EXPERT ?

Maybe not, but they sure know how to make you ask for relationship advice..

Google: Top asked relationship questions?

It could be early in the morning or even late at night and someone somewhere in the universe is Googling a question about their relationship. Lets face it, we want answers anyway that we can get it. This is how Google became apart of our lives.

This is chapter is merely for the laughter, but check out some of these relationship questions that individuals are searching on Google and the responses are simply hilarious.

According to Date Report's writer Miri Rosen in an article that she wrote in the year of 2013 individuals are googling for relationship advice and it is funny as hell. It surely made moi laugh! The things that we ask Google and let us not forget Siri.

"What the hell are people thinking when they Google these relationship questions"

Have you ever personally started typing a question in the Google search engine and way before you finish, Google has helped you to finish with its own suggestion? Of course you have, we all have Googled a question. I know that I have. Below are some of these questions that others have Googled. Check them out. This is so funny!

1. Is my girlfriend pregnant?

Have you had sexual relations with that woman? Was it not just in the Bill Clinton way with her under a desk? Were either of you as short-sighted as our former president, and not use protection? If you answer "Yes" to any of the above questions, there might be a visit to Planned Parenthood in your future. Their waiting rooms are supposed to be great, though!

2. Is my girlfriend attracted to me?

Your girlfriend *was* attracted to you. That's how she got to be your girlfriend. Is she still attracted to you? I don't know. Maybe you should try asking her instead of Google? Make sure to wear your fanciest sweater when you do!

3. Is my girlfriend bipolar?

No. If you stopped being a jerk, worrying whether she's pregnant and finds you attractive, she wouldn't have mood swings that you have dubbed "bipolar." That's not even a nice thing to ask.

4. Is my girlfriend controlling?

Concentrate and ask again.

1. Do girls like facial hair?

The short answer is yes. The longer answer is yes and yes.

2. Do girls like muscles?

Yes. But if you in any way resemble a bodybuilder, absolutely not. And stop taking those steroids.

3. Do girls like abs?

Yes. Abs are a muscle and we have determined that girls like muscles.

4. Do girls like skinny guys?

Are you constantly eating and still skeletal? If so, that's decidedly unfair and no. But there are probably still plenty of girls that will bone you, you skeleton, you.

1. Do women have prostates?

Have you taken a science class?

2. Do women have wet dreams?

Only when they dream of you.

3. Do women like beards?

See "Do girls like facial hair?" You think you're all cool because you can grow a full beard and you go for real "women," not "girls"? Well then. You're totally right. You are cool.

4. Do women come?

If you're asking this question, the answer is, "Probably not with you."

1. Do men have one less rib?

Yessiree, and snakes talk and your older son is going to kill your younger son.

2. Do men like virgins?

Most guys are freaked out by it; others are turned on by it. Whatever floats your boat.

3. Do men get yeast infections?

Yes, but it's called jock itch, so it sounds vaguely virile and more appealing.

4. Do men like tall women?

Super model tall, yes; Julia Child tall, no. But a good man will like you no matter what size you are. Awwww.

1. Is dating haram?

Seeing as Palestinian women just got license to troll the internet for Muslim loving, I'd say no.

2. Is dating your cousin wrong?

The next thing you should Google is "local psychologists specializing in incest."

3. Is dating biblical?

Are you trying to say that Abraham wasn't a great date? Because he was.

4. Is dating a numbers game?

Everything is a numbers game, including dating. But remember, it only takes one. And one is the easiest (and loneliest) number.

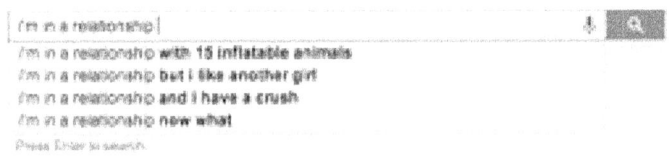

1. I'm in a relationship with 15 inflatable animals.

Wow, that seems very difficult to maintain. Do the animals get jealous of each other?

2. I'm in a relationship but I like another girl.

Don't beat yourself up. It happens. Be nice to both of them, because they deserve it.

3. I'm in a relationship and I have a crush.

On your significant other? How sweet! Keep that love alive.

4. I'm in a relationship now what?

Maybe invest in 14 other inflatable animals

Google is only one of the things that todays generation is doing to get at that chick or guy, there is texting, sexting, snapchat, hitting them in the DM on Instagram, Facebook creepers lurking on their prey. This is why I don't feel bad when someone gets tricked by someone with a fake page on Facebook. Why are people falling for these scams. A little advice, don't be Facebook desperate. There are creeps in the world and some of them are online. Individuals spend their time online, they have lost the ability of face-to-face communication. We talk to Siri. We want answers anyway that we can get them. This is just the age that we are in.

    I remain to be old school. My approach has been different. I have not communicated with someone in a relationship via online, but I do know many others that have done so. Online dating is popular. Lets face it, even if it does not work. Individuals still like the option of being able to communicate with individuals from all over the world without having to leave their home. Google has tapped into a line of communication to reach consumers and they continue to grow with the people. Go ahead and Google it.

Chapter 16

IF YOU HAVE THE PRIZE, SHUT THE F UP

You have the partner of your dreams, in fact he or she comes home to you every chance they get but you keep running your mouth about outside forces that are irrelevant. So what if he has a baby Momma, so what if she has a baby Daddy -you are the one who has the prize. Stop spending time worrying about someone who lost. If they lost, they lost for a reason. No worries! We have all been there worrying about some female or some dude that holds no weight in our partners life. Trust moi when I say that if you have him or her that 9 times out of 10 the ex is not even an issue. In fact the only thing that they have on your partner is the fact that they have a child with them, they know this. They know that this is the only thing that they can use to even get his or her attention. Period.

    The real issue is not the ex, the real issue is the fact that there is a lack of self confidence in knowing that you are handling your business. When you handle your business you will see the results that you desire. Handle your business without the negative attitudes, the controlling spirit, the drama, and the non stop accusations which is the real reason that you feel like you may be losing your partner.

    It is so important that you find the reason for your own insecurities, majority of the time they come from a past pain, failure, or something tragic that happened to you that you have not let go of yet.

We enter into new relationships with old problems, which is sad for the person that we are with who is being punished for something that they have never ever done to you. We speak negative to our partners until they reach a point of being fed up with it.

Our lips are for speaking greatness and life into the lives of one another. Our lips are not for the tearing down of the person that we say that we love. Anytime you are being negative on a regular basis, along with a constant verbal abuse against your partner you may want to re-evaluate your love for them. You may not even love them, you may be infatuated with the idea that they bring to the table. Not to mention that you don't even feel worthy of having him or her that is why you have not accepted the fact that he or she just wants to be with you.

Contrary to what we have heard or even been taught, there are some faithful partners in this world. We all can experience loyalty and faithfulness when we truly fall in love. Real love has no fear in it. The more you understand real love the less you should operate under or in fear. Love lacks the consumption of all fear!

Afterword

We all desire to have a Happy Ending in our lives and that is perfectly ok. Living life is so awesome when you get in tune with your own god or goddess body. You will find out that there is not only more to life, but there is more energy life for you. Trust in the love that is within you, it will lead you in the right direction.

    Start living life for the greater you and the best part of you will come to the light. Expect to have the happiest ending and you will have just that. This book was written at first with moi in mind. I had my own issues, things that I wanted to understand, and then I realized that it was not about moi. Writing this book became about releasing the hope that we all are able to love again after all of the bullshit. We are still able to live a happy, fruitful life, and we are able to do so in peace. Love does win, you have to be the one who allows love in, and most importantly it is necessary that you are the one who trust in love. Don't forget that there is more to Happy Endings, this is only Vol I in Vol II you will enter into my *43 Confessions of a Love Goddess*. I can't wait. See you there!

Author Bio

*B*orn December 29, 1979, in Ouachita Parish, Louisiana. Humes was raised in a small home in the country side of Epps, Louisiana by her grandparents-Sarah & Al Humes. Where she saw two separate individuals love one another as one. This gave her a foundation to build upon until life challenged her to understand what that truly meant in the terms of 'true love.' This is how Humes became a hopeless romantic at heart. As painful as her journey in love has been she has never given up on the fact the the truth about love and relationships exist in each each one of us.

Today she combines her love for family, life, beauty, fashion, lifestyle traveling, and writing to living her dreams to the fullest. Life Coach, Designer, Brand Consultant and Author of Success is What You Make it & The PR Plan, Founder of Luxury PR Boutique-RBR PR & Advertising Agency, Moghul Life, Inc, Tri'ex Legacy, Inc, Humes Luxury *Intl*. along with many other of her boss endeavors. Humes purpose is to reduce poverty, provide jobs for as many individuals as possible, and to guide and lead the next generation into leadership. Currently she is residing in the US.

YES FOLLOW MOI

CONNECT WITH MOI:
It remains a goal of mine to connect with as many individuals as possible. I shared important parts of my life, not because I felt like there is anything new to be taught but that each one of us has a different message to deliver. My goal is to write as often as I can, to share with you the ups and downs of my life, and to inspire you to have hope to keep going regardless of what your situation looks like. The spirit of God is the only thing that kept moi going and still keeps moi going when the rest of the world tried to show moi otherwise. I pray that I have imparted something in your spirit. I hope that Happy Endings puts a smile on that face of yours.

SOCIAL MEDIA FACE BOOK / IAmMonisoiHumes **TWEET MOI** @mhumes **IG** @monisoihumes **LINKED IN** in/monisoihumes **YOU TUBE** /user/soilifestyle **ITUNES** Soi Lifestyle **PINTEREST**/monisoihumes

Other Titles Available

Happy Endings: The Godly Version

ISBN-13: **978-0692629994**
ISBN-10: **0692629998**

Happy Endings Vol II/ 43 Confessions of a Love Goddess

ISBN-13: **978-0692629987**
ISBN-10: **069262998X**
Family & Relationships / Love & Romance

The PR Plan {The ultimate guide to owning your own brand}

ISBN-13: **978-0692403754**
ISBN-10: **0692403752**
Business & Economics / Public Relations

Success is What You Make It

ISBN-13: **978-1492305781**
ISBN-10: **1492305782**
Self-Help / Personal Growth / Success

References

Bible/ King James Version/I John 3:18. Print

Chapman, Gary. *The Five Love Languages, Secrets to love that lasts*. North field Publishing, 2009. page 60. Print

http://www.statisticbrain.com/dating-relationship-stats/

http://AshleyMadison.com
http://CougarLife.com
EstablishedMen.com
Avid Dating Life
Avid Life Media

McLeod, Calum. www.usatoday.com/story/news/world/2015/03/04/china-one-child-policy-births-beijing/24069319 March 4, 2015

Kendrick, Stephen, Nixon, David. *Fireproof*: United States, Sherwood Pictures, Affirm Films Films: September 26, 2008

http://fireproofthemovie.com

Amorous, Sophia. Girl Boss. Portfolio, Reprint Edition, September 29, 2015, Print
http://girlboss.com/SophiaAmoruso/
http://nastygal.com/about-us/

m.imdb.com/title/tt1000774/ 2008 SexintheCity/Film/2008/Director/MichaelPatrickKing/ Writers/MichaelPatrickKing, Candace Bushnell, Darren Star

http://www.tantra-kundalini.com/nadis.htm

http://www.biography.com/people/kim-kardashian-450760#growing-up-in-beverly-hills

http://www.huffingtonpost.com/entry/the-10-most-common-complaints-sex-therapists-hear-from-couples_56203b85e4b06462a13b8494

http://internet-filter-review.toptenreviews.com/internet-pornography-statistics.html

Ambrosini, Diane, http://www.livestrong.com/article/78078-definition-prana/. Live Strong. Feb 18, 2015. Article

Mindful Muscle, http://www.mindfulmuscle.com/loving-sexual-energy-kundalini-meditation/

http://www.hermes-press.com/spiritual_energy.htm

www.ingramcontent.com/pod-product-compliance
Lightning Source LLC
Chambersburg PA
CBHW070146100426
42743CB00013B/2824